Annely Karron Art

PORTRAITS

By Annely Karron

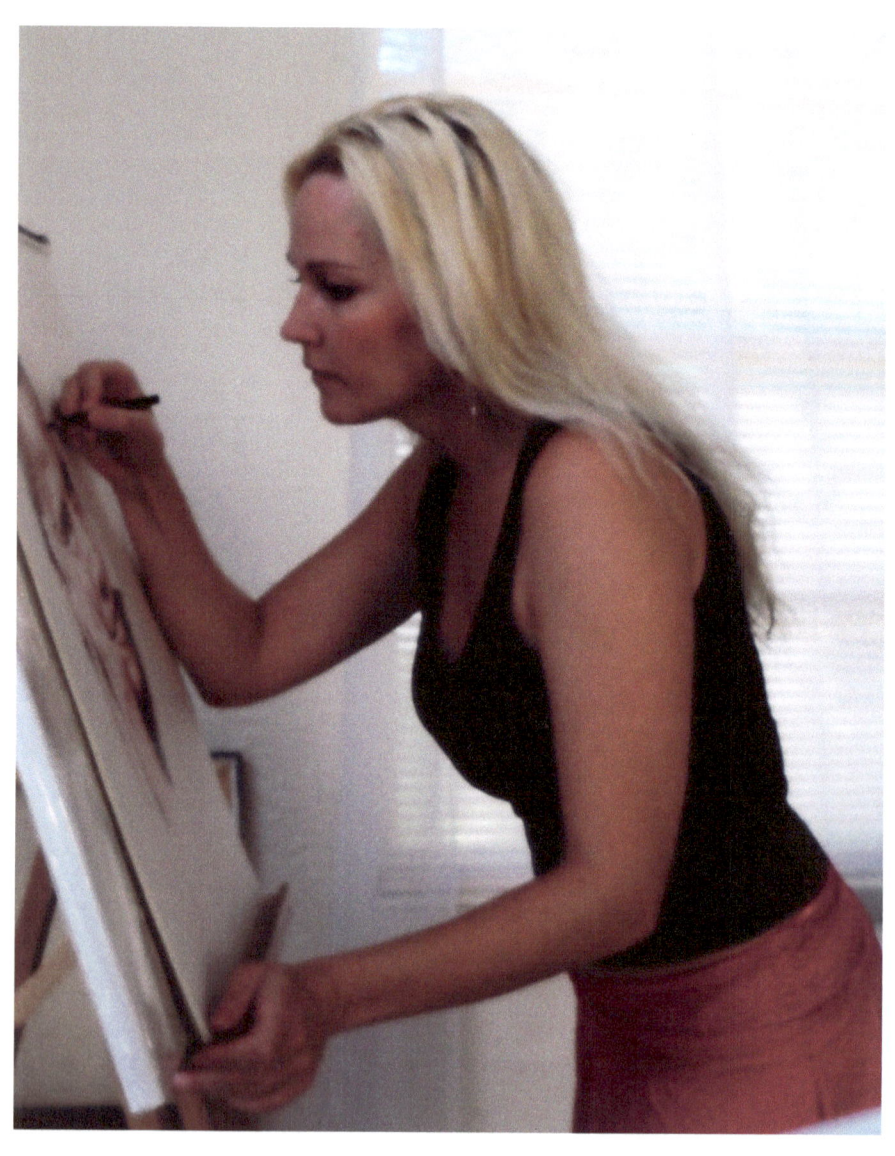

Copyright © 2018 Annely Karron

All rights reserved.

ISBN-10: 172766907X . ISBN-13: 978-1727669077

Dedication

This book is dedicated to all art lovers and the ones who enjoy creating portraits themselves.

I put together a collection of very old portraits (created when I was a teenager) and some I have done over the last few years for clients, including friends and co-workers.

Most of my portraits are done using pencils or color pencils but I have also used oil-pastel, wax, markers and acrylic paint.

I have done portraits in ACEO sizes (2 x 3") and life size portraits.

Hope you will enjoy!

ANNELY KARRON ART - PORTRAITS

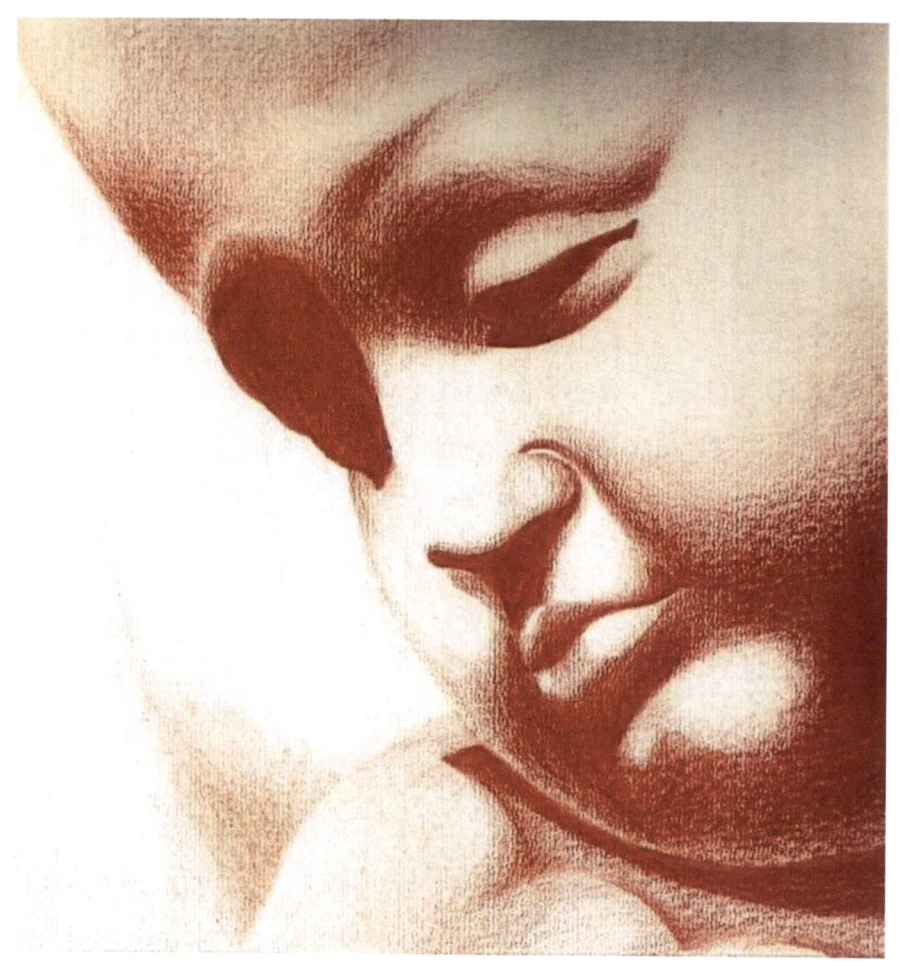

Color Pencil - 1990

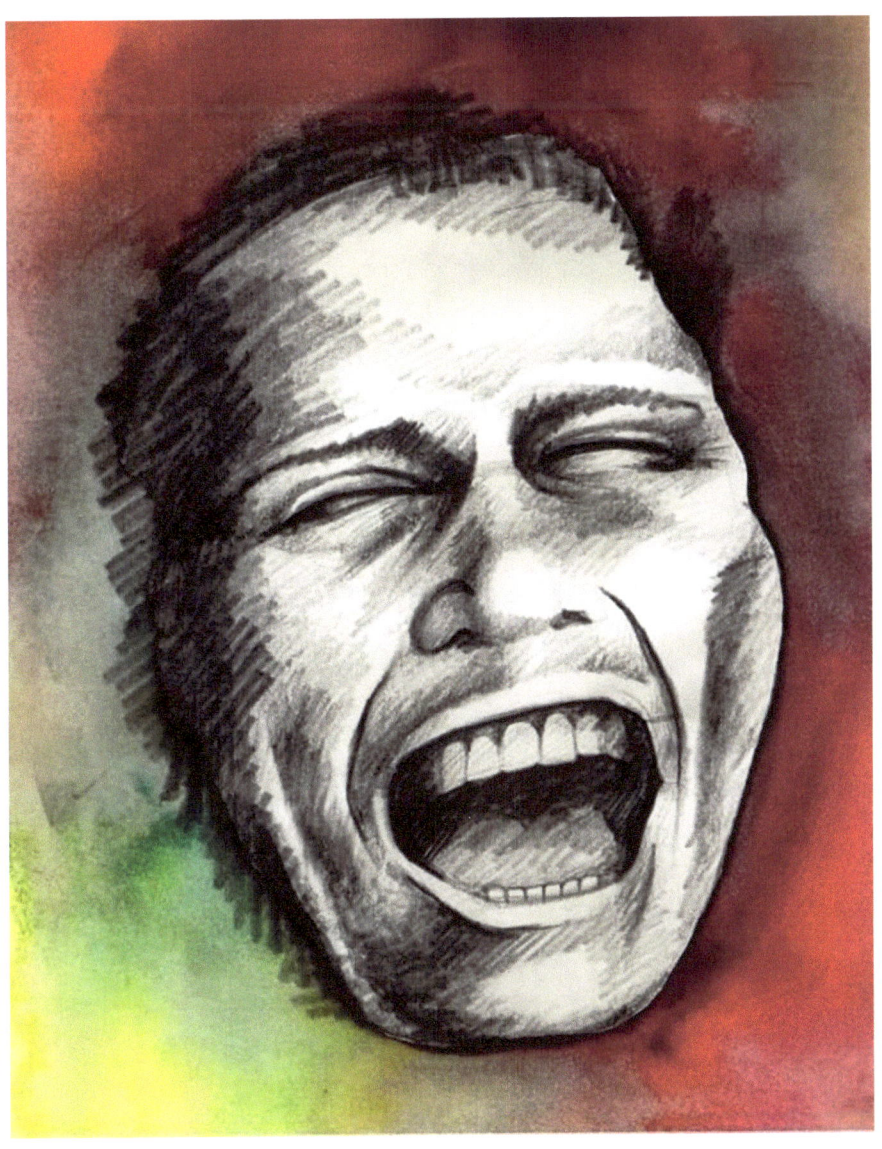

Pencil and Water Color - 1995

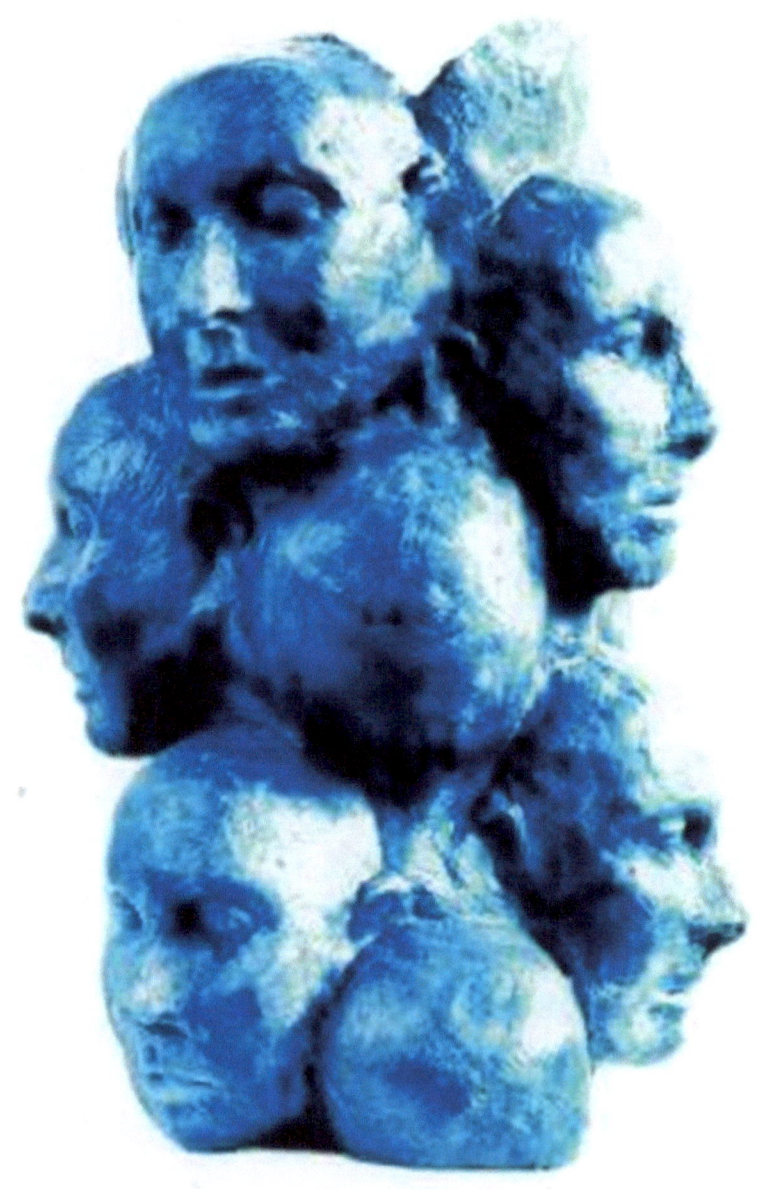

Wax - 1998

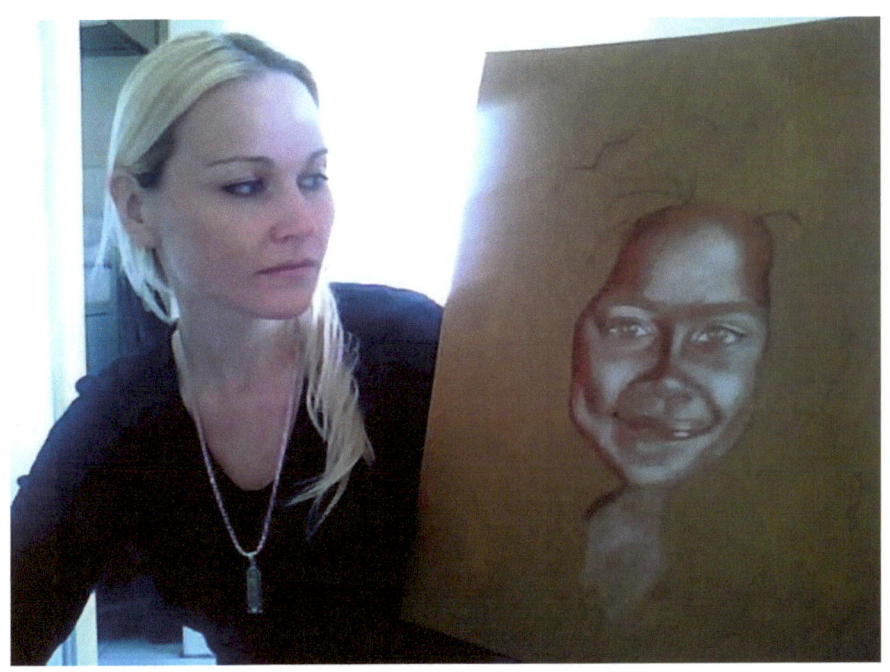

Work In Progress

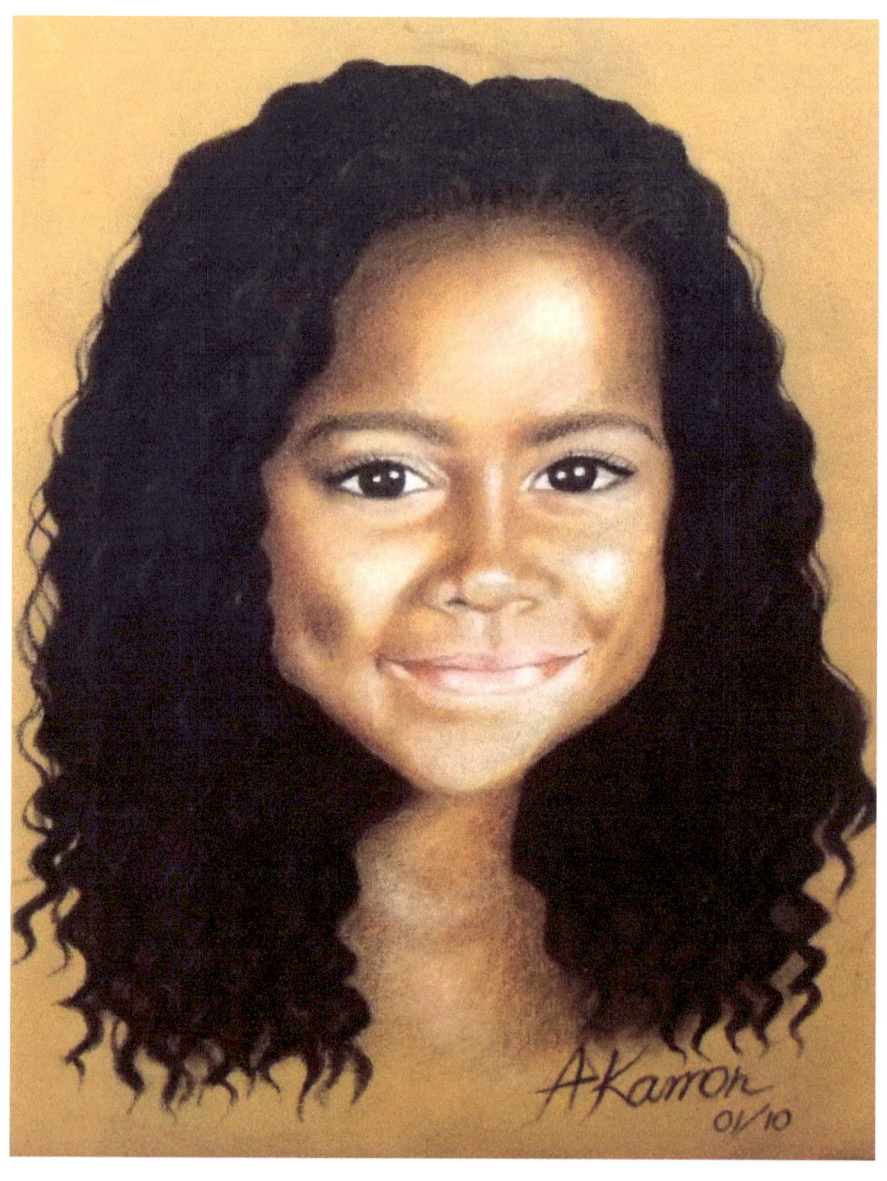

Color Pencil on Canvas Board – 2010

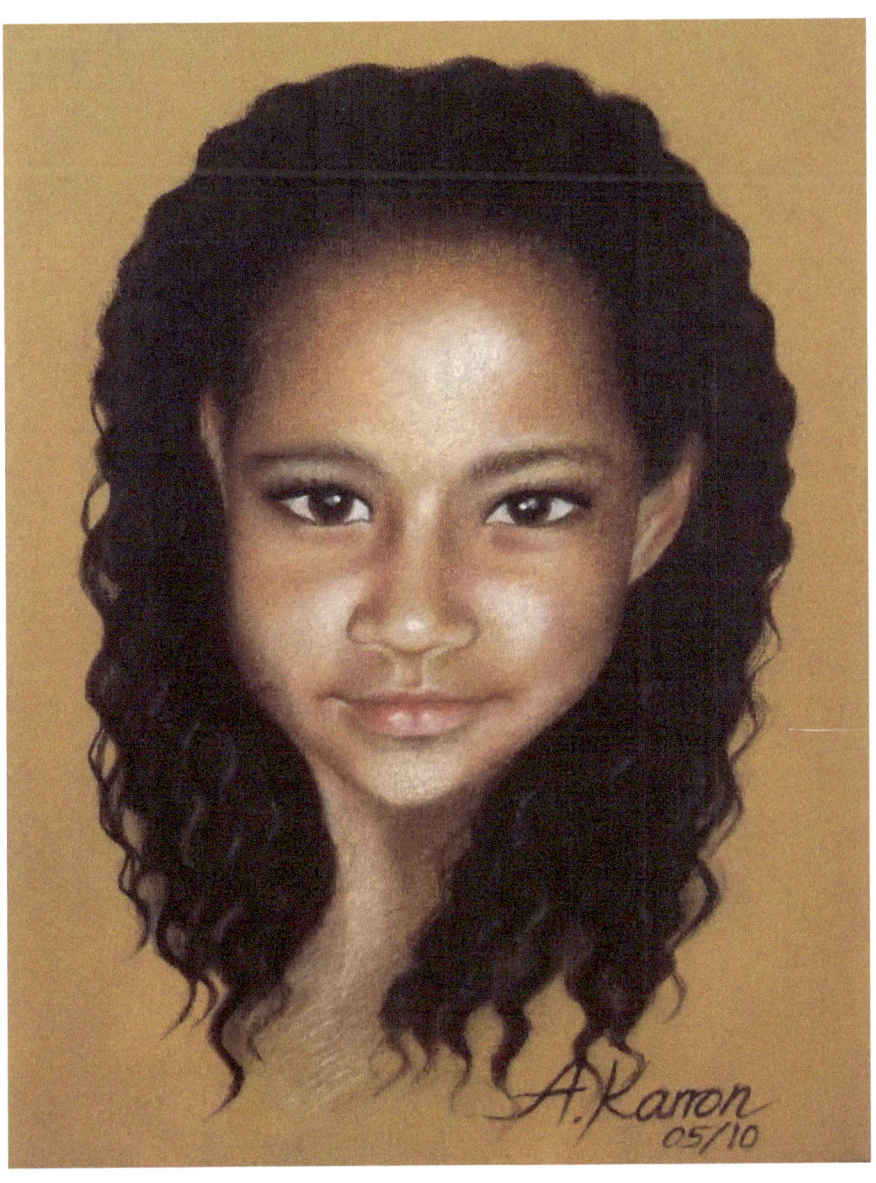

Color Pencil on Canvas Board – 2010

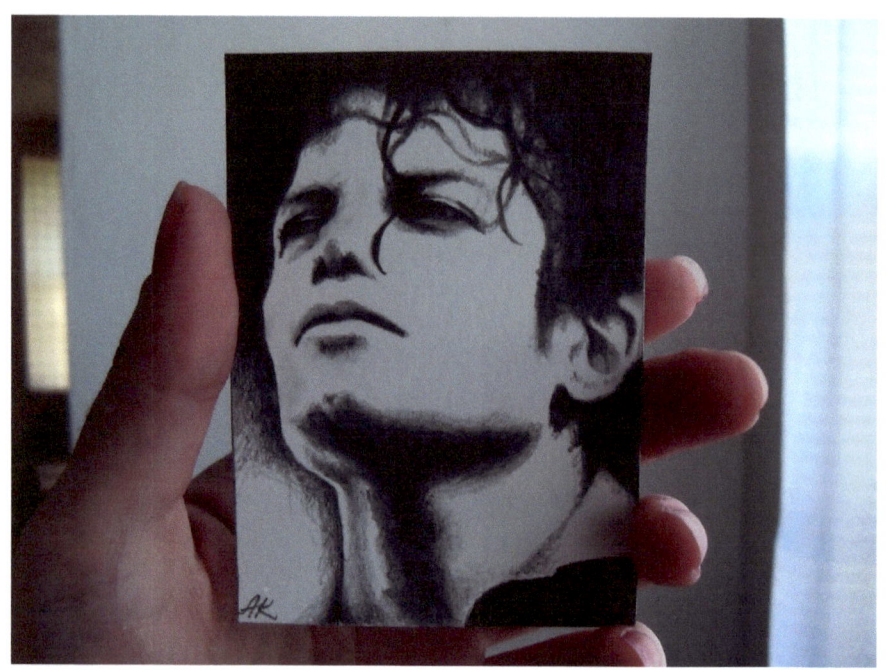
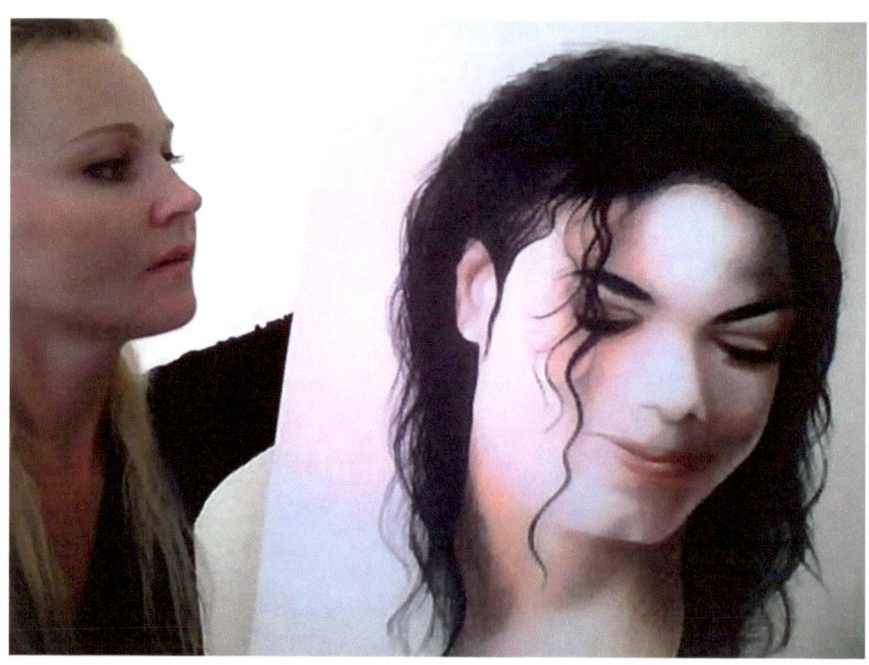

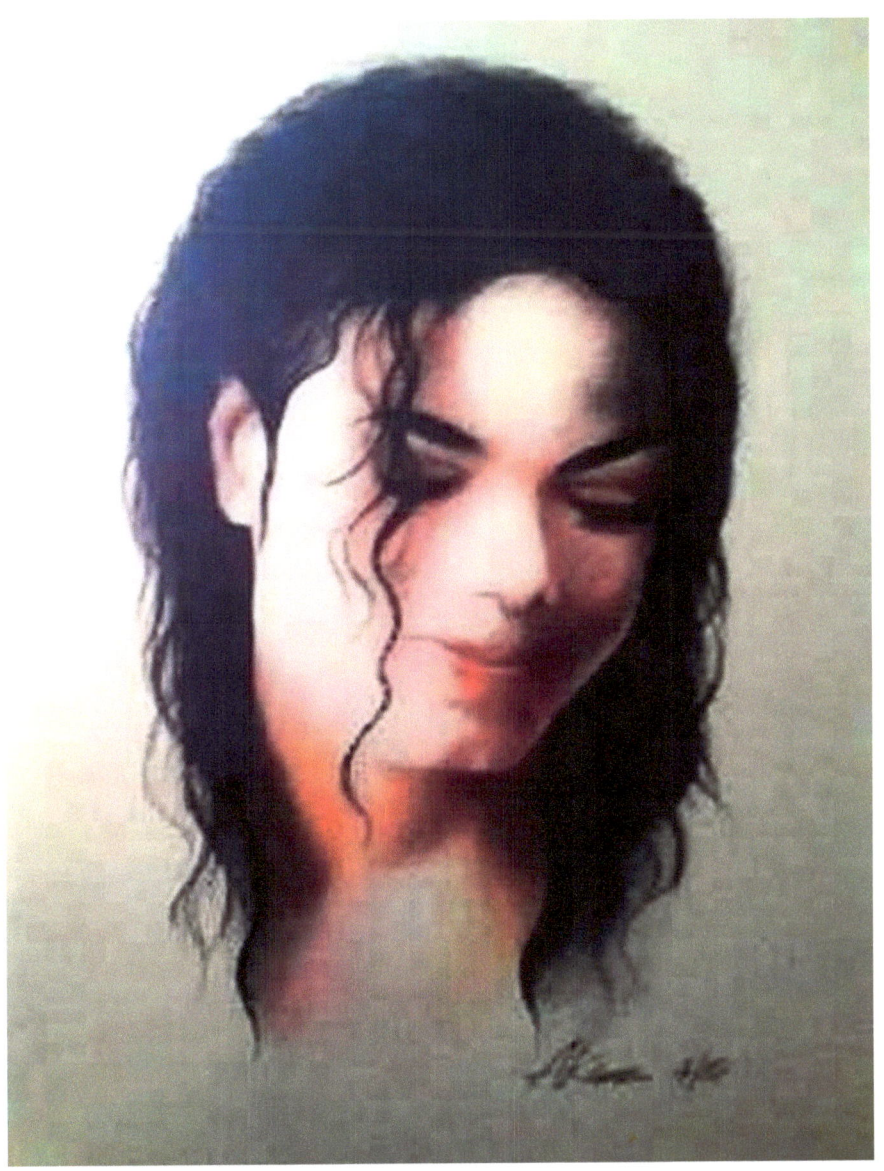

Color Pencil - 2010

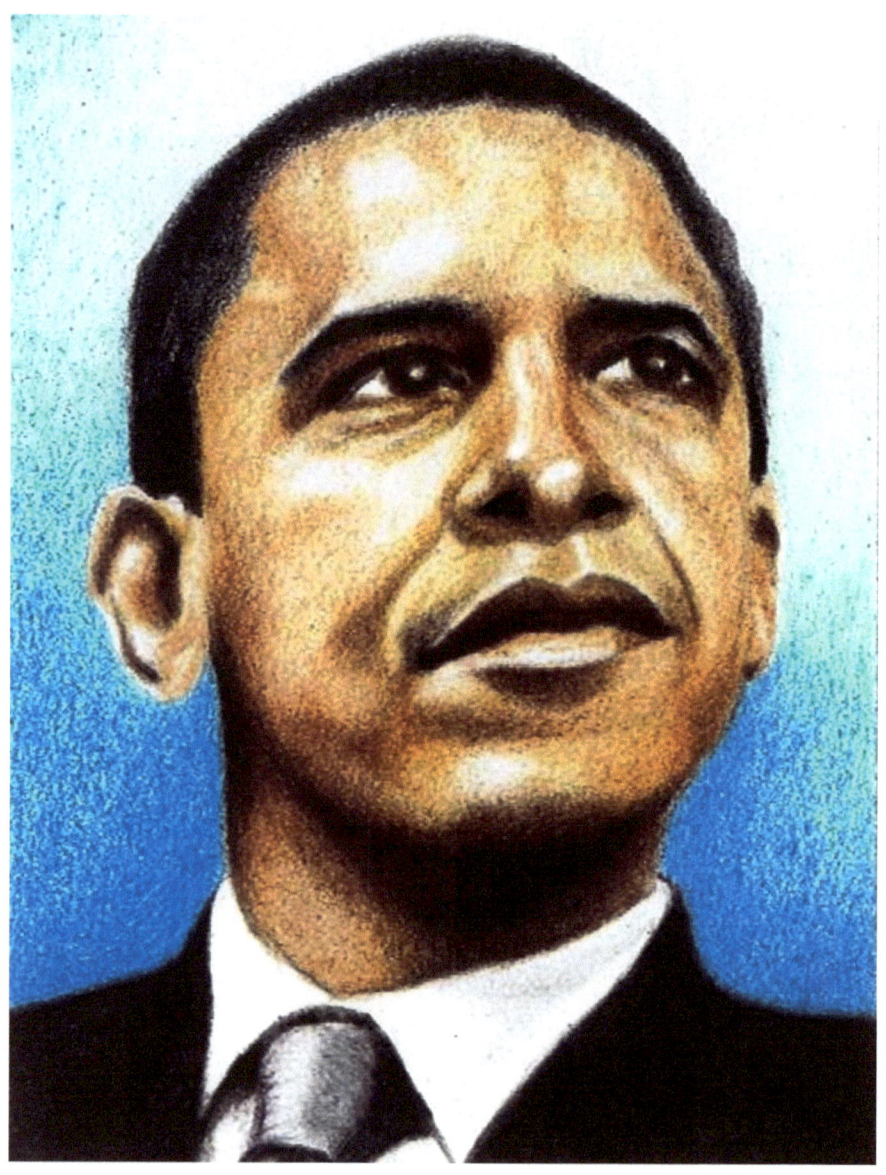

ACEO – Color Pencil

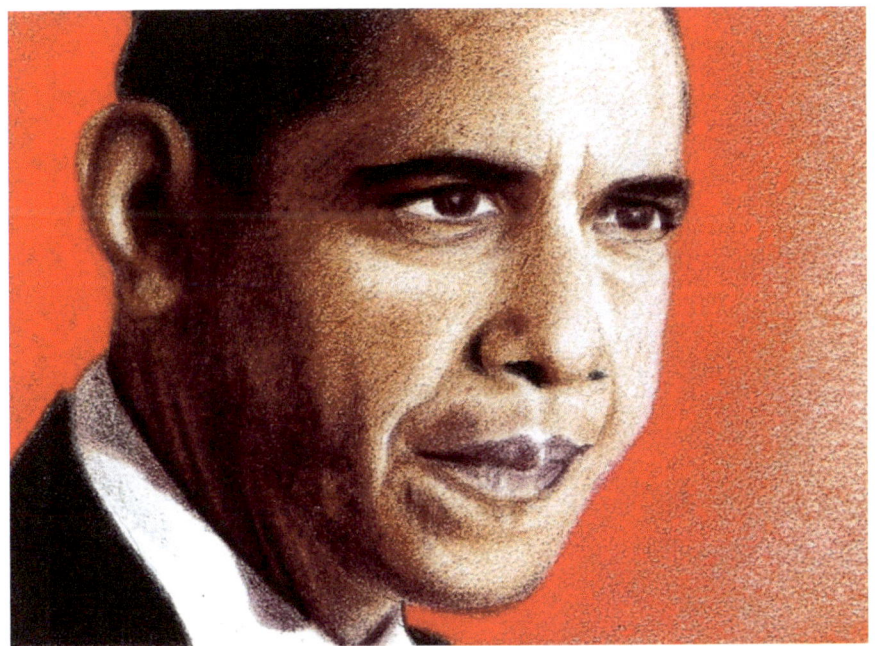

ACEO – Color Pencil

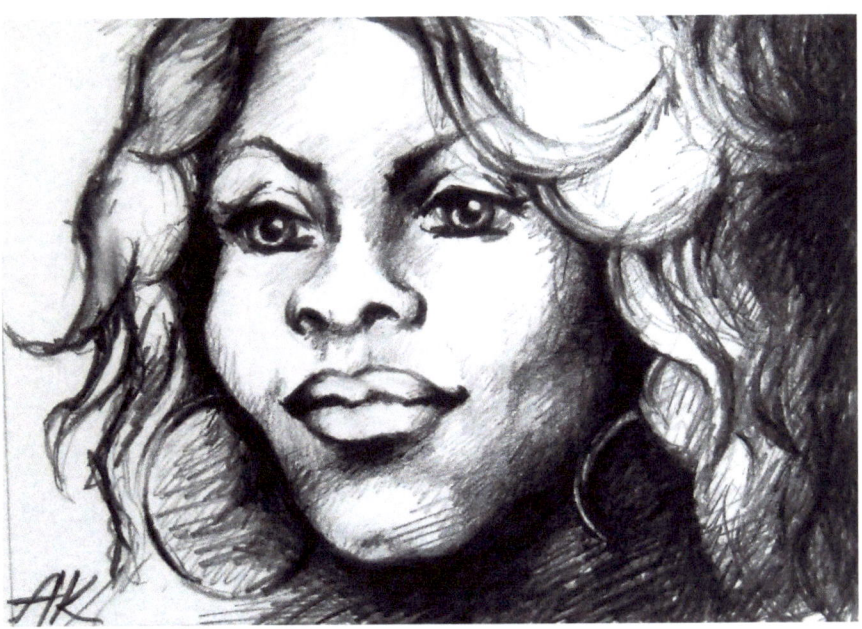

ACEO – Pencil

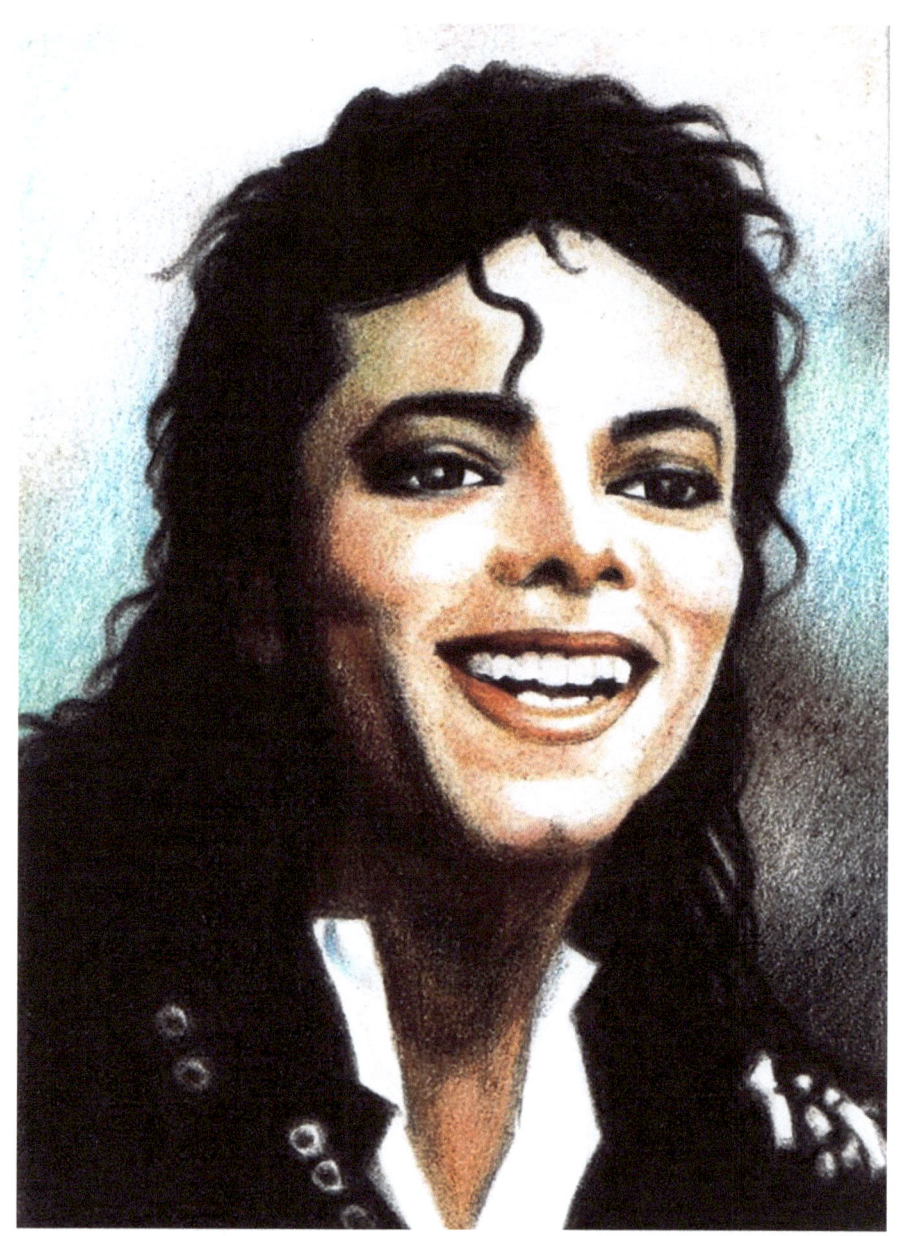

ACEO – Color Pencil

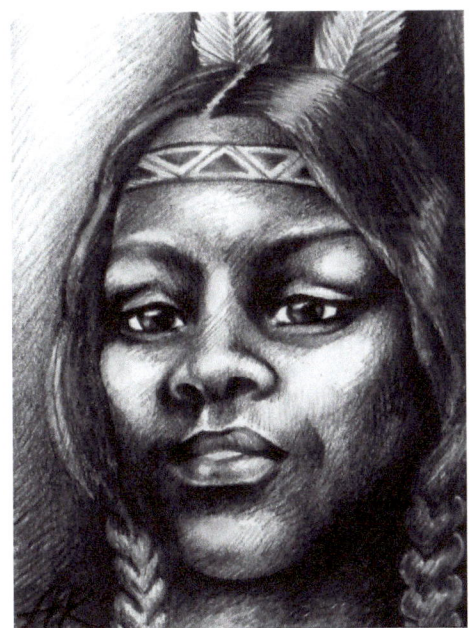

ACEO - Pencil

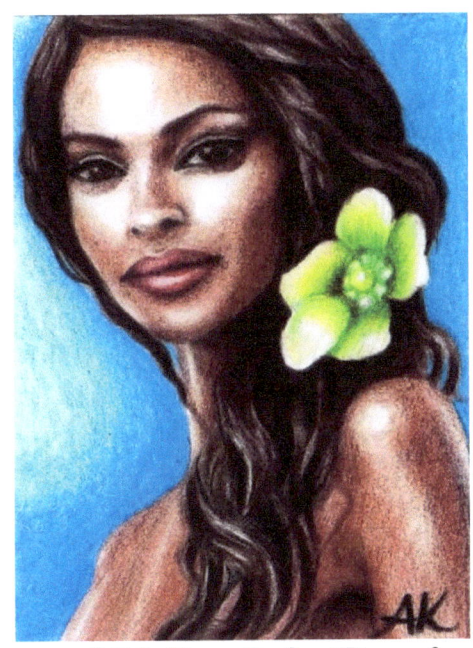

ACEO – Color Pencil

ANNELY KARRON ART - PORTRAITS

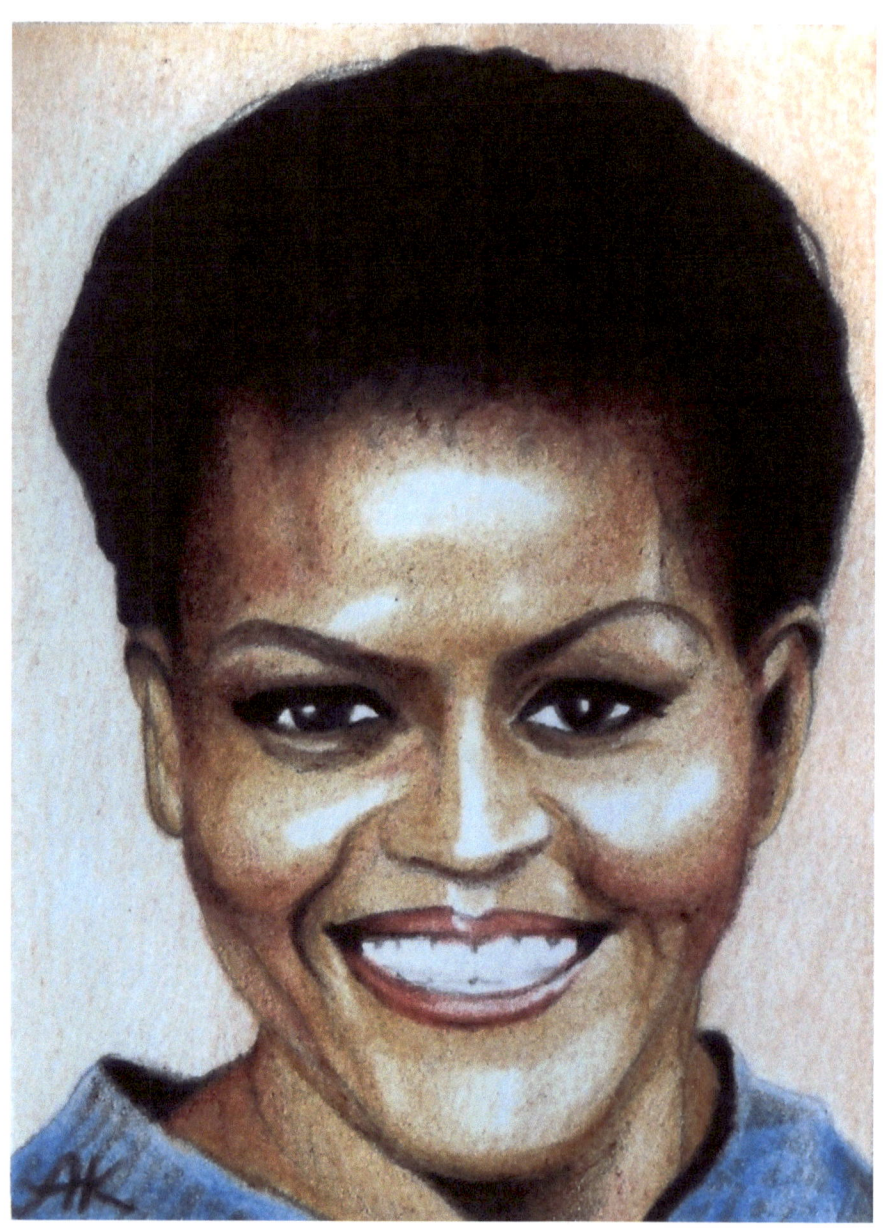

ACEO – Color Pencil

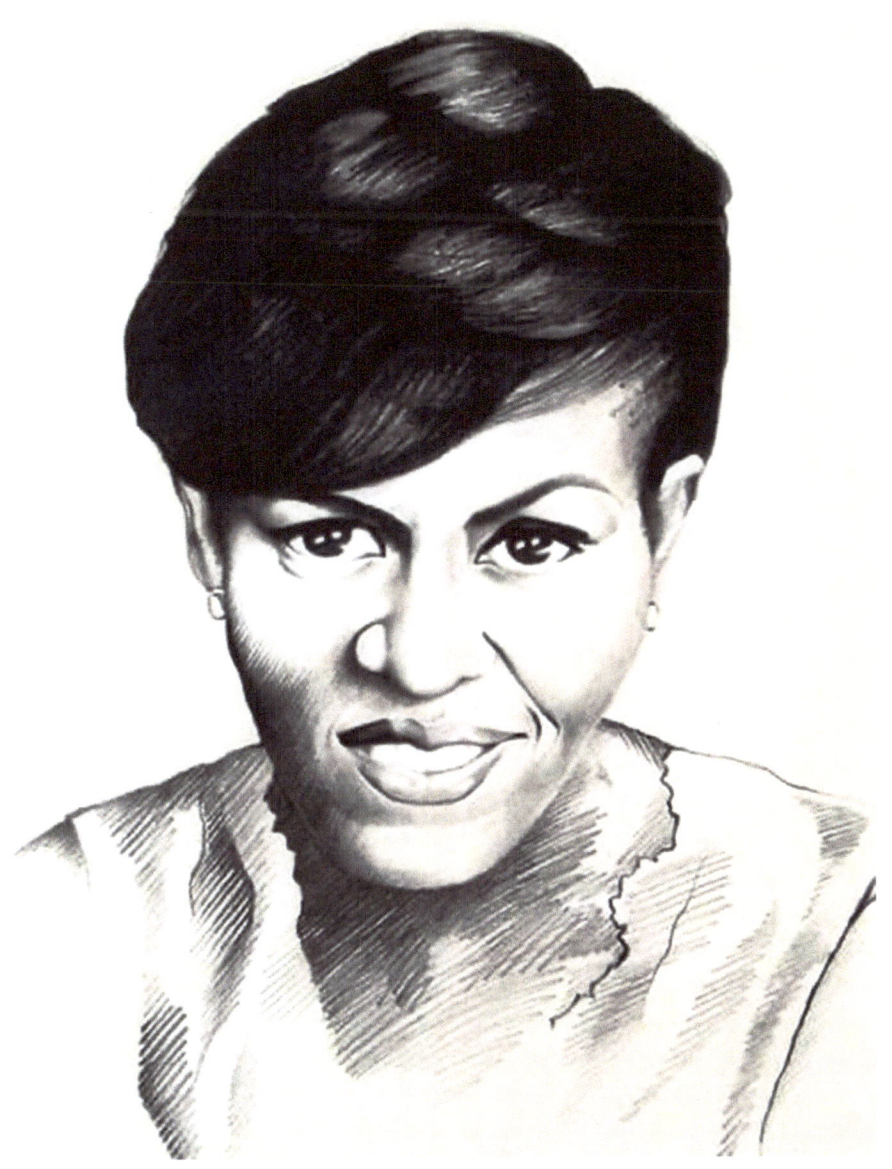

Pencil Drawing - 2010

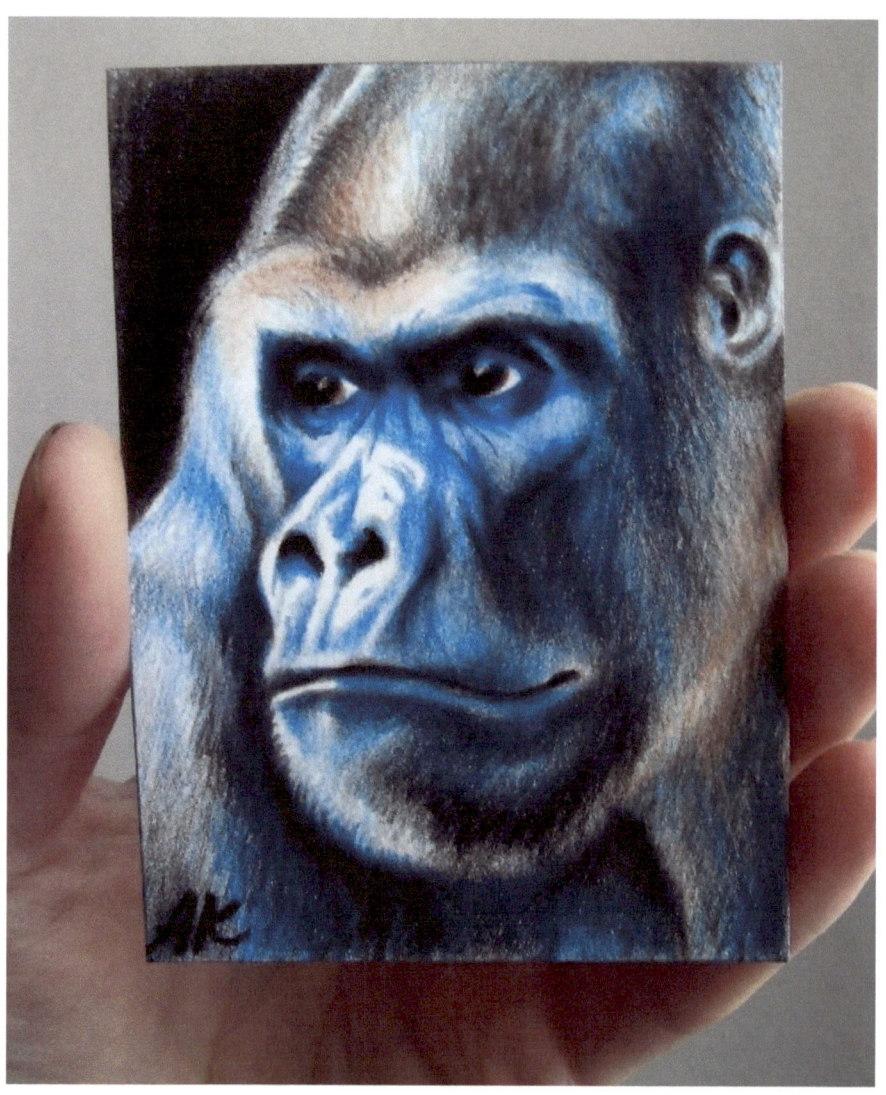

ACEO – Color Pencil

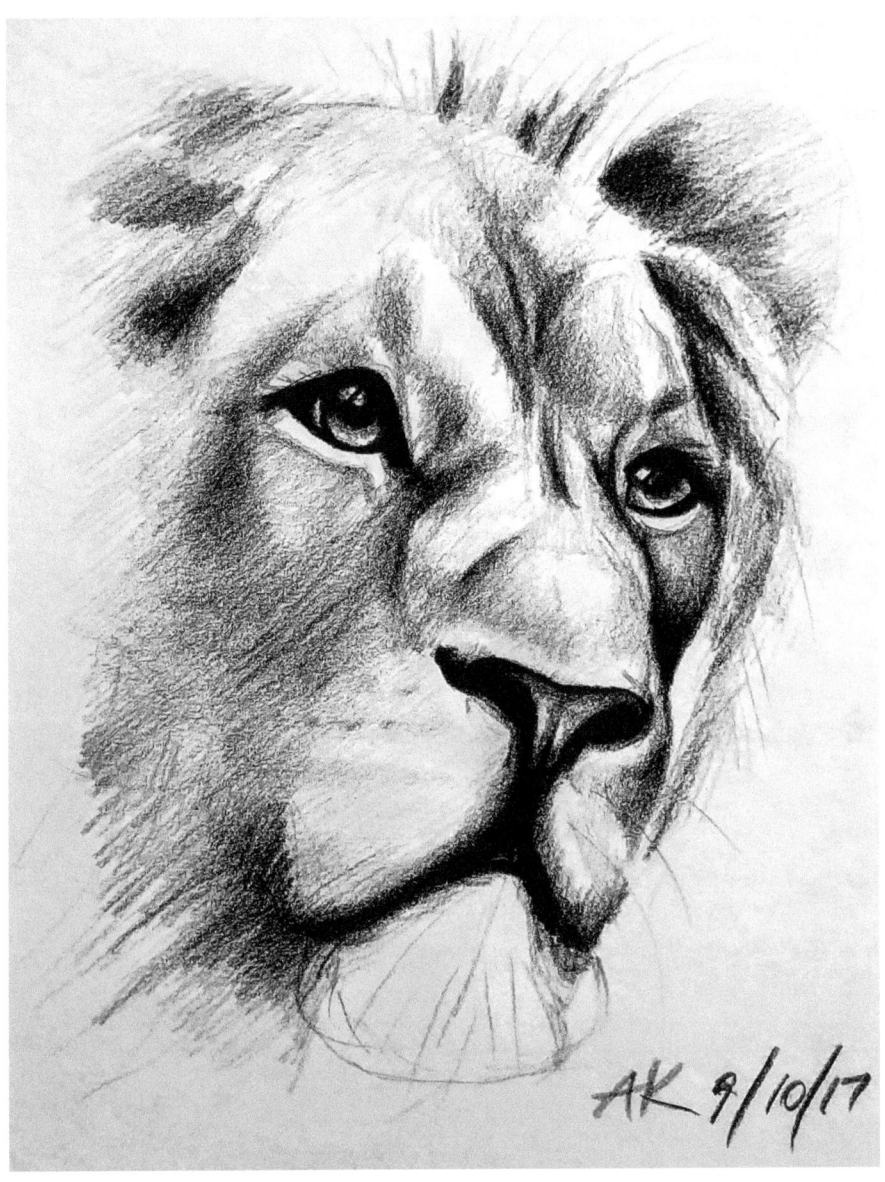

Color Pencil Sketch - 2017

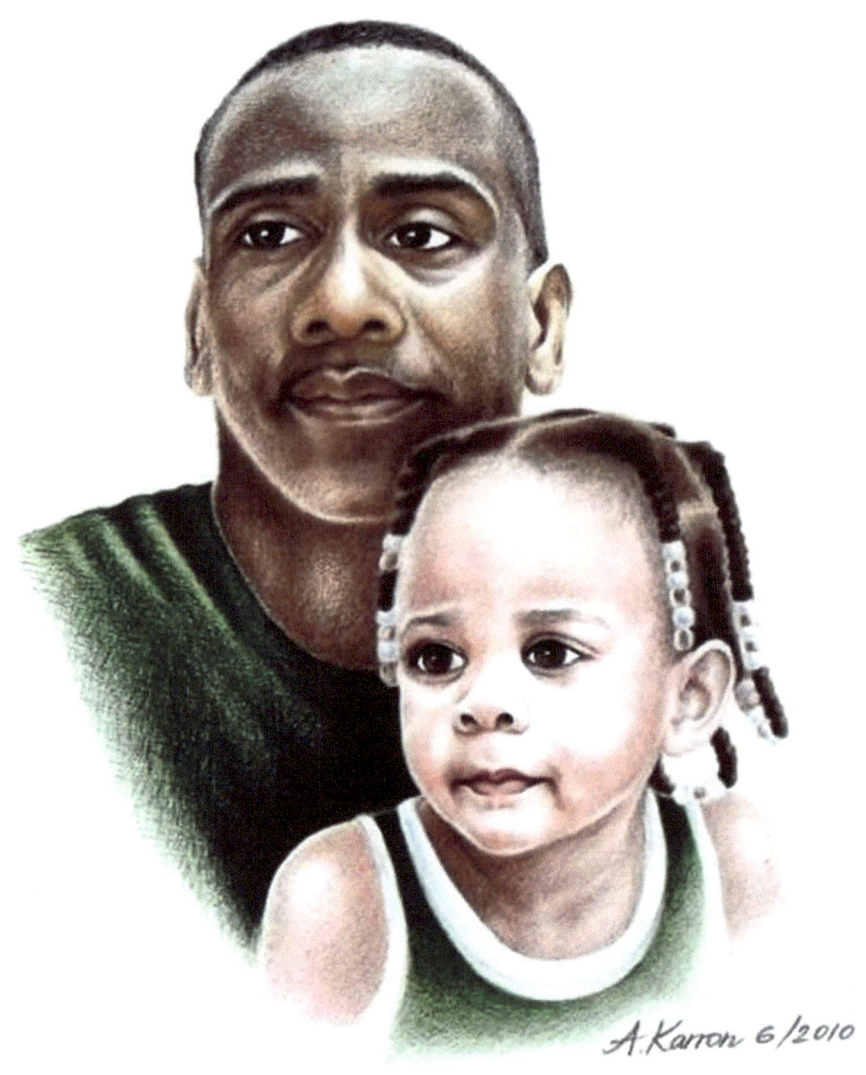

Color Pencil - 2010

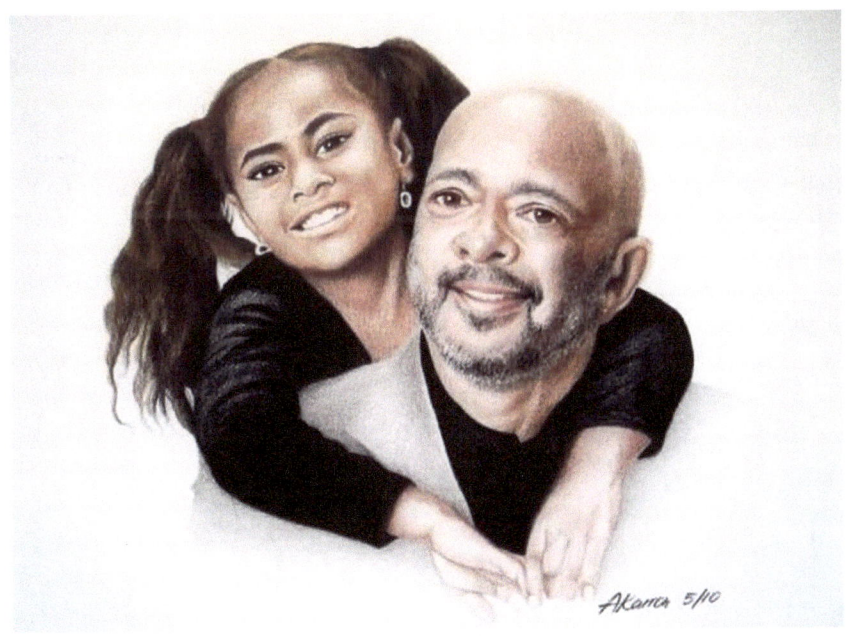

Color Pencil 2010

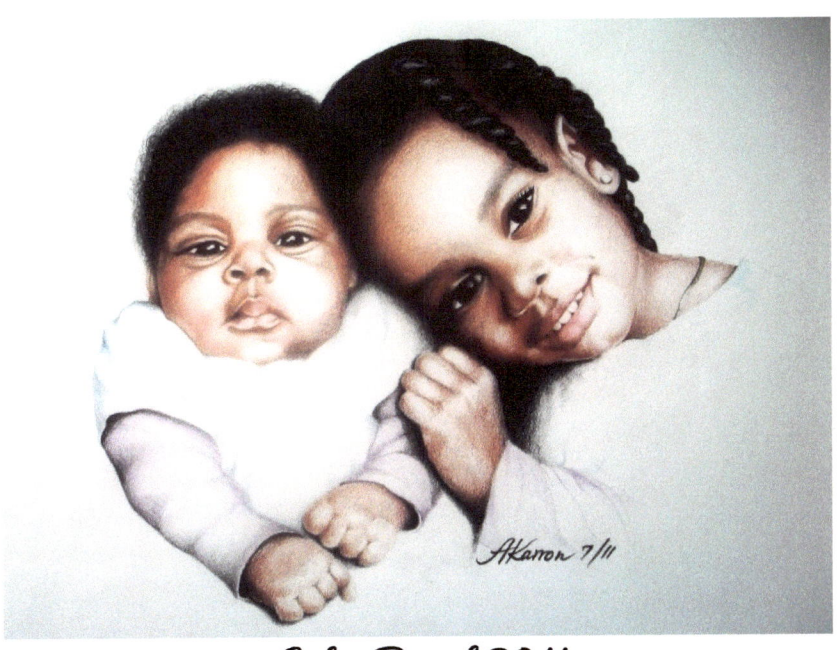

Color Pencil 2011

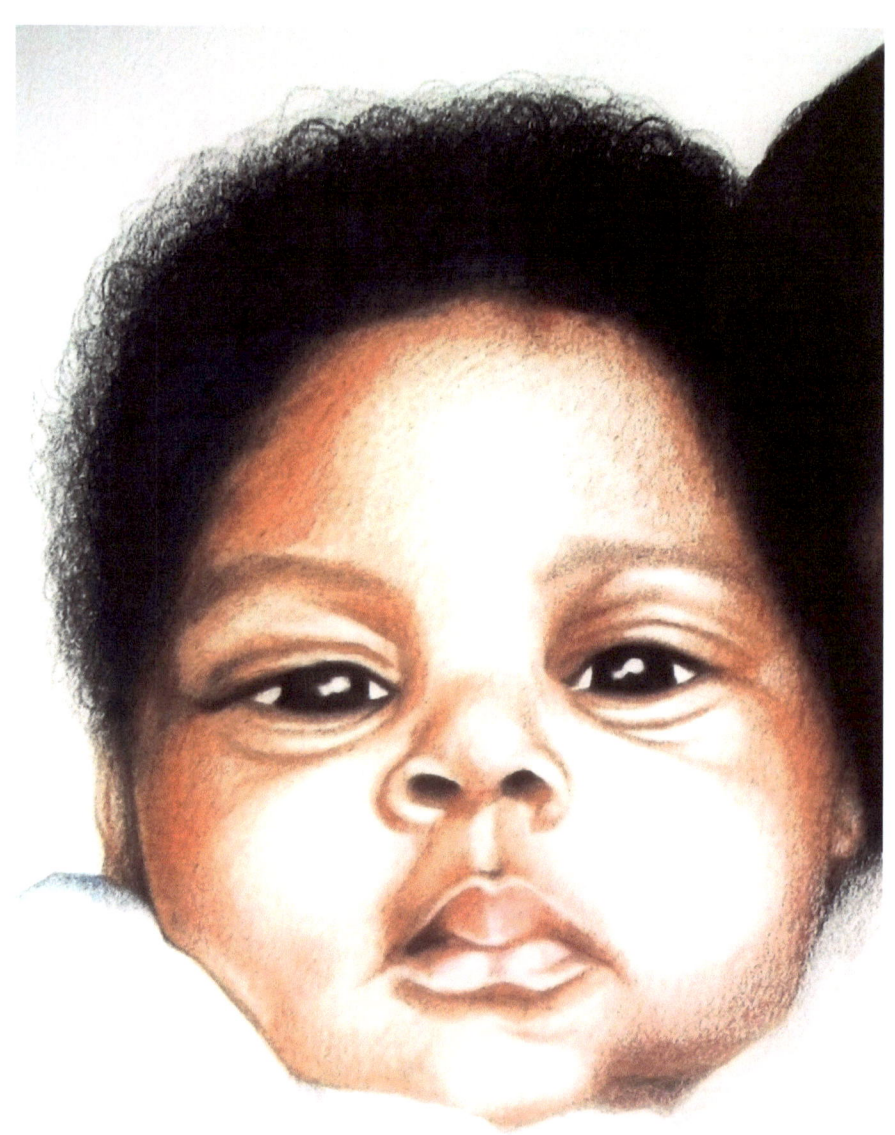

Close Up – A

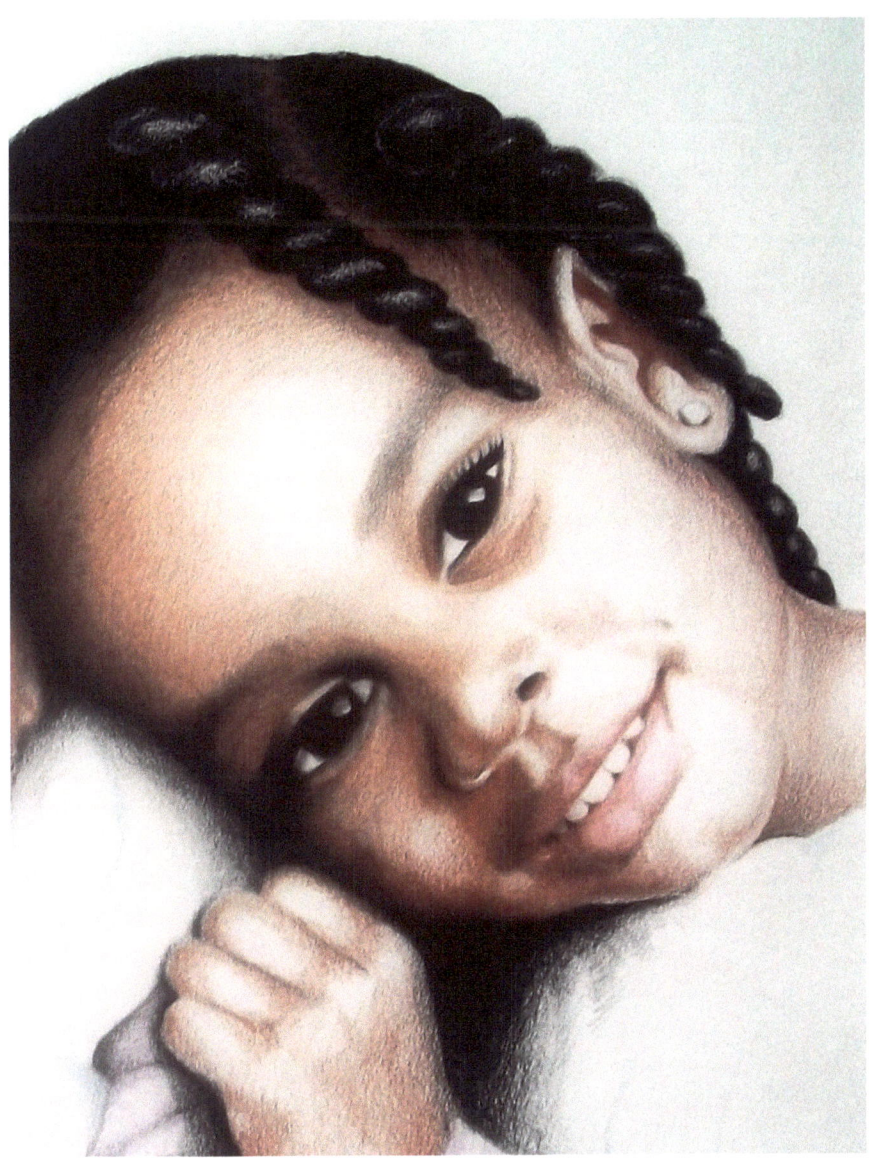

Close Up - B

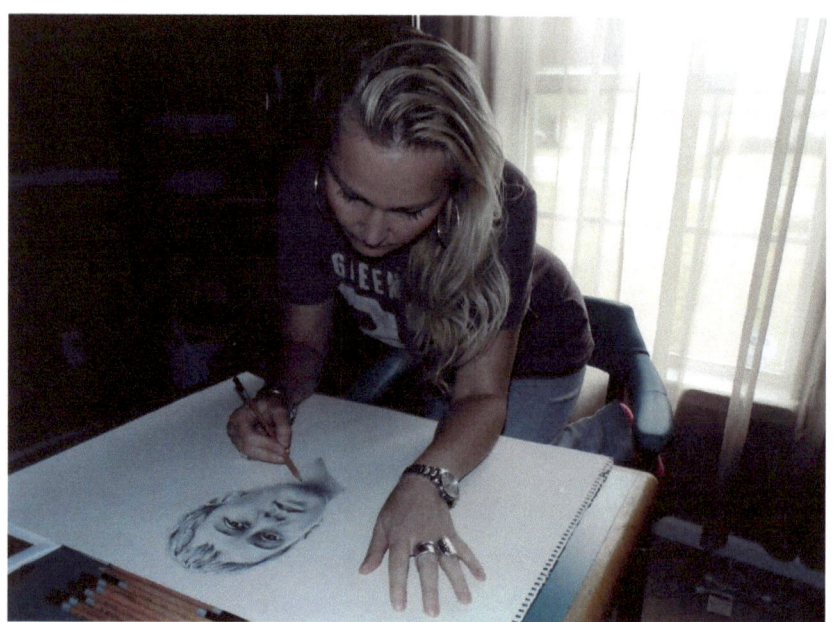

Work In Progress

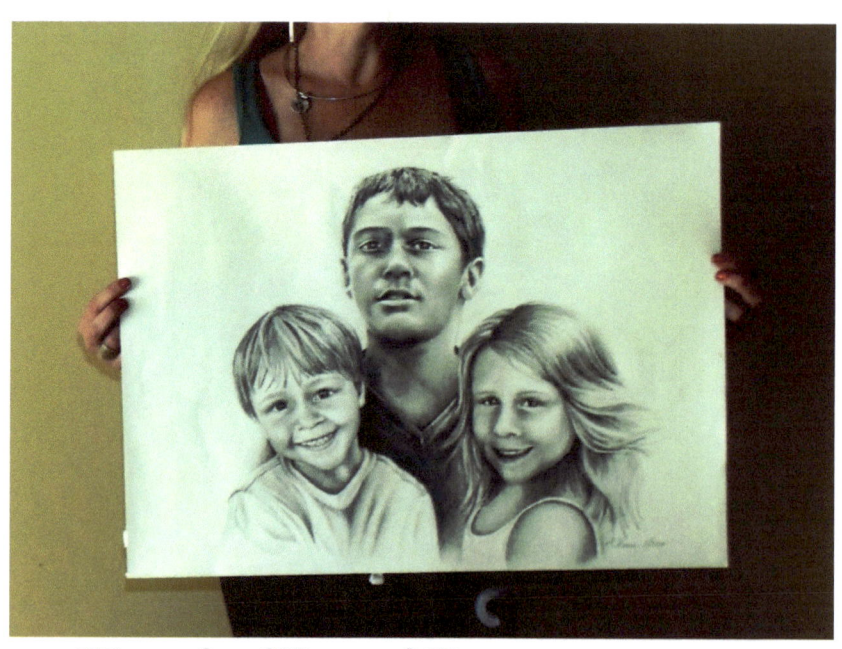

Finished Pencil Portrait - 2015

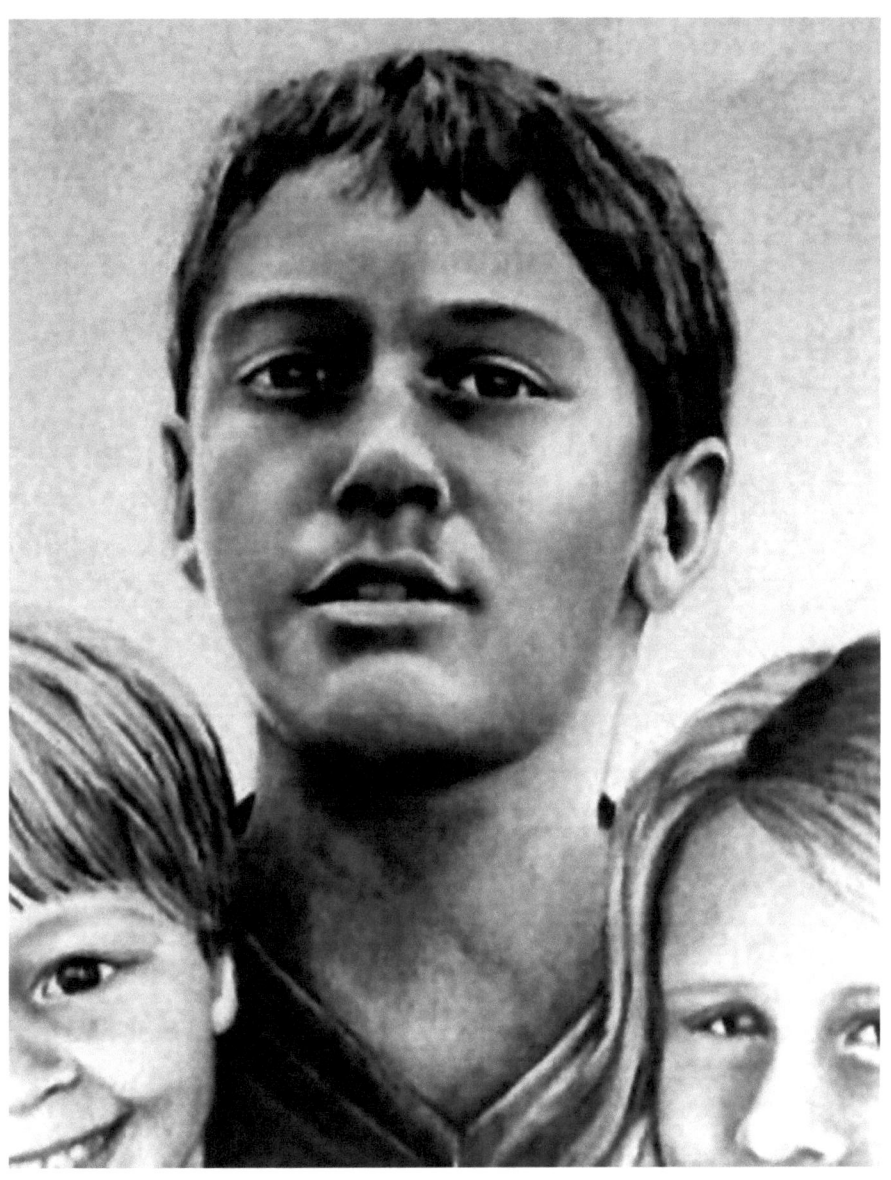

Close Up

ANNELY KARRON ART - PORTRAITS

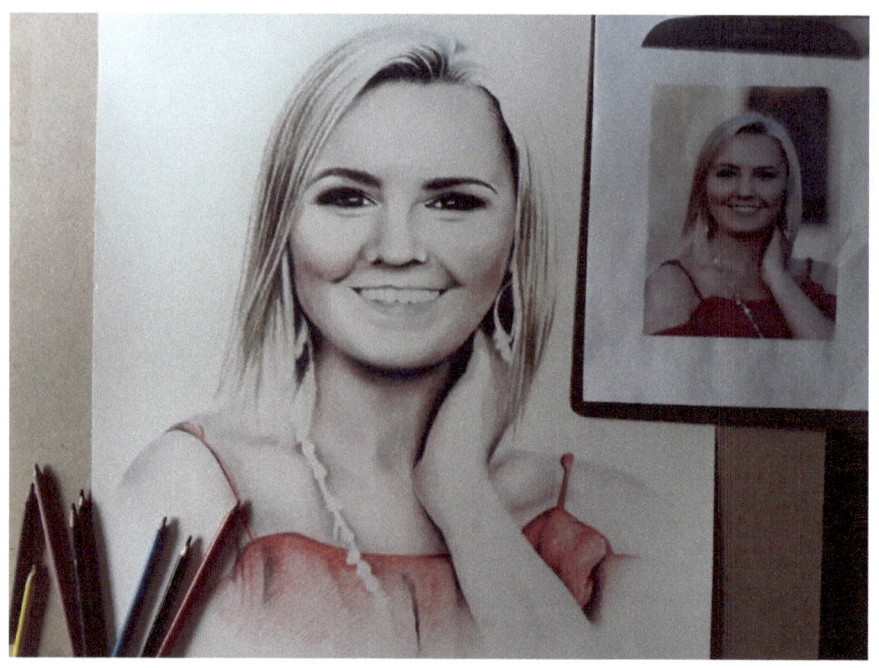

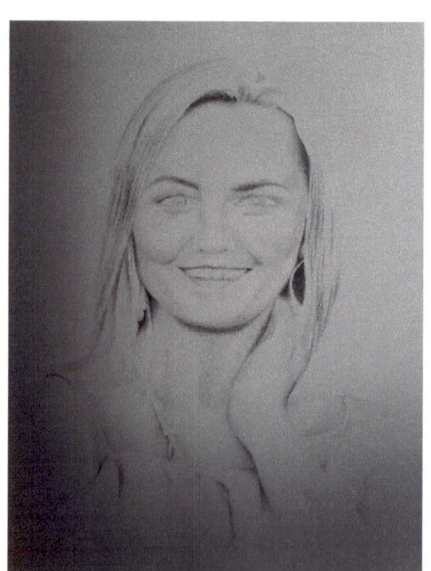

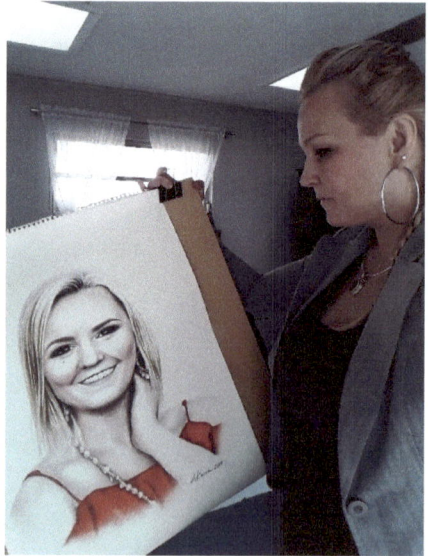

Work In Progress

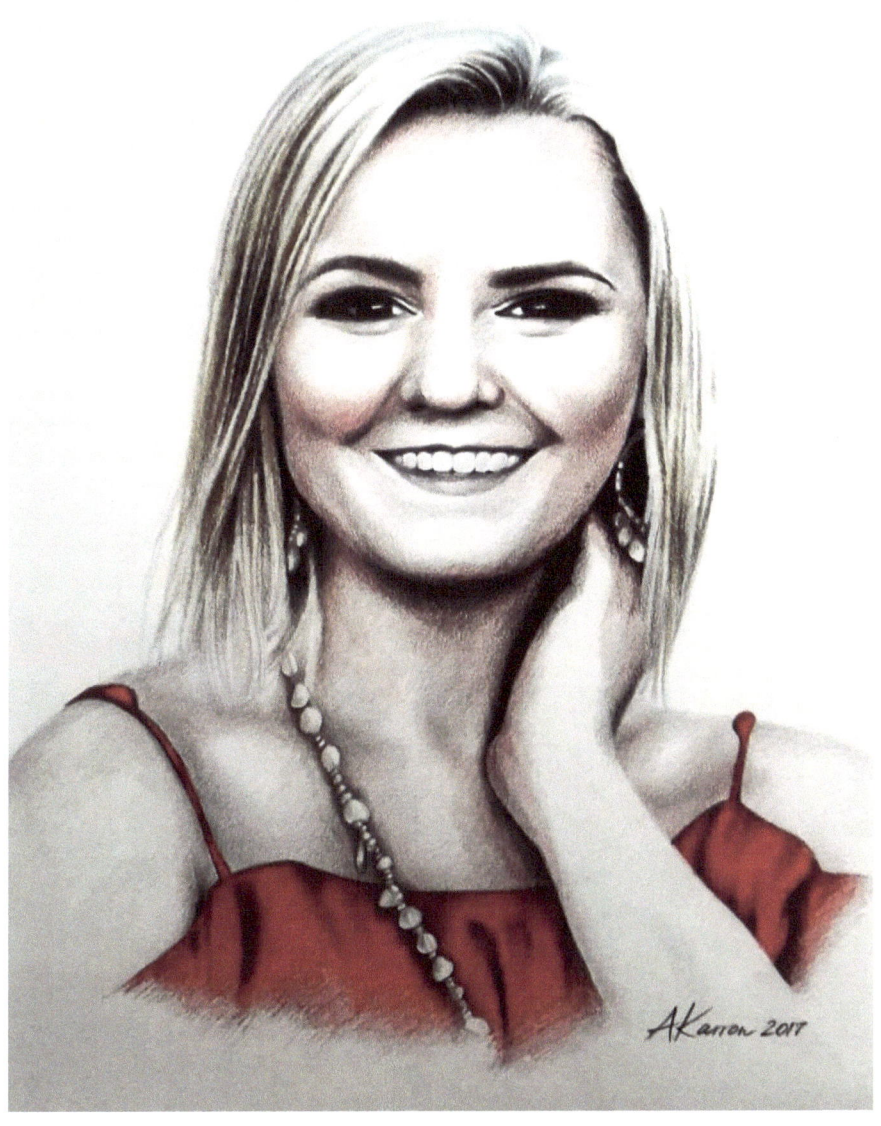

Finished Portrait Color Pencil - 2017

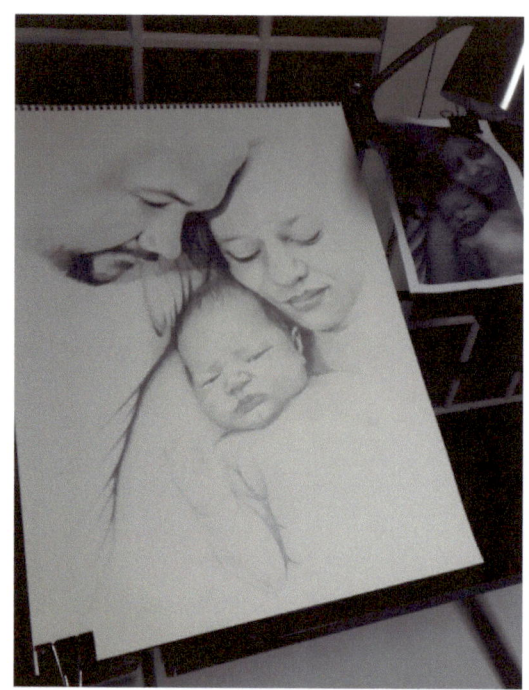

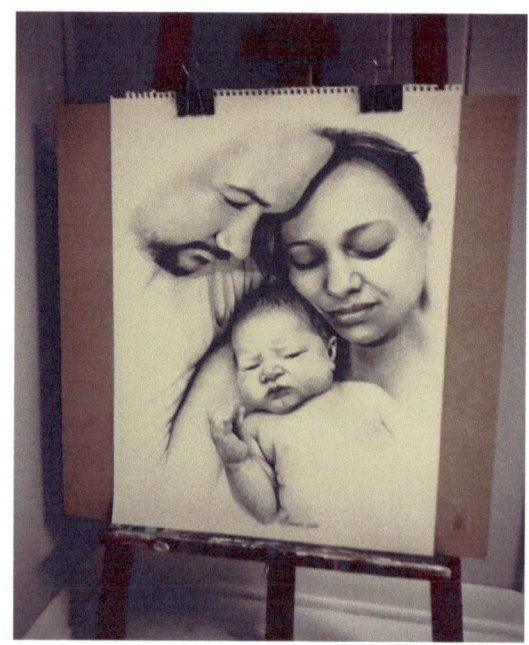

Work In Progress

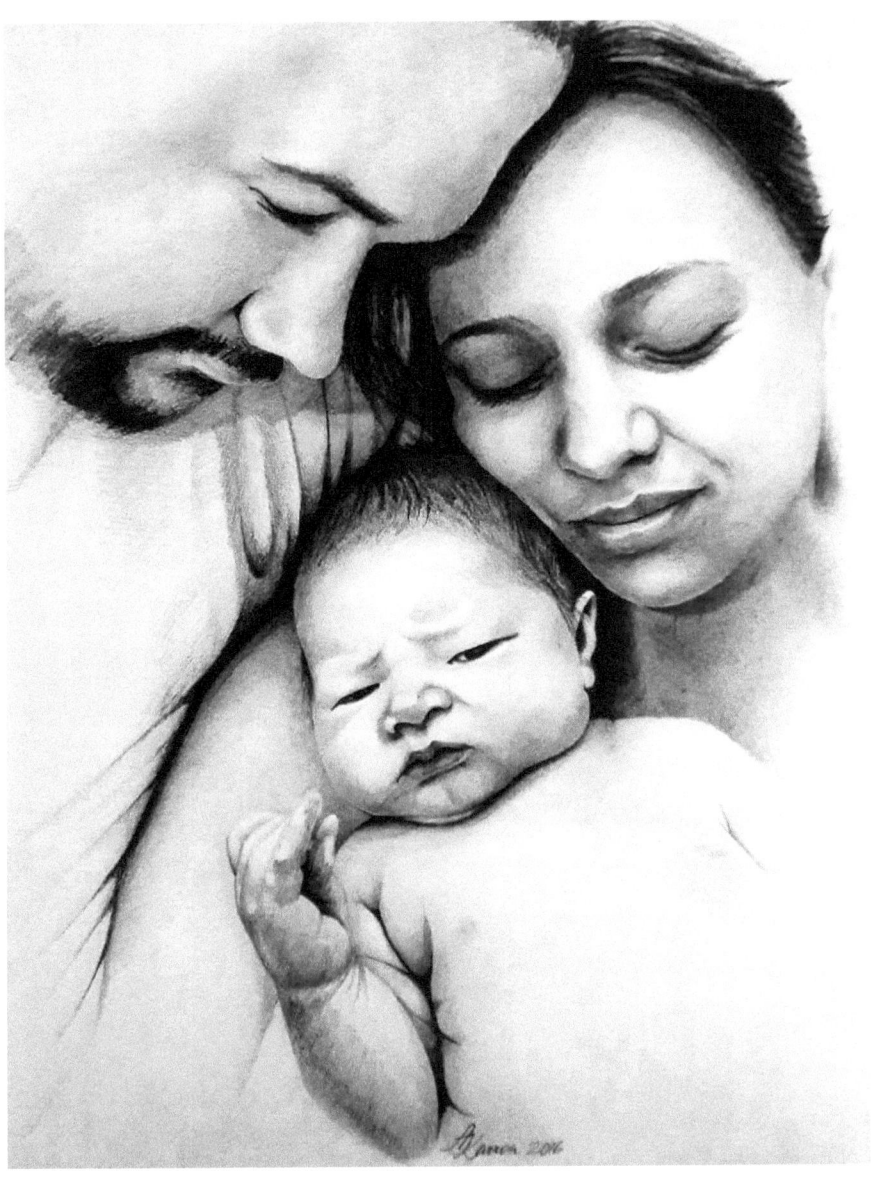

Finished Pencil Portrait - 2016

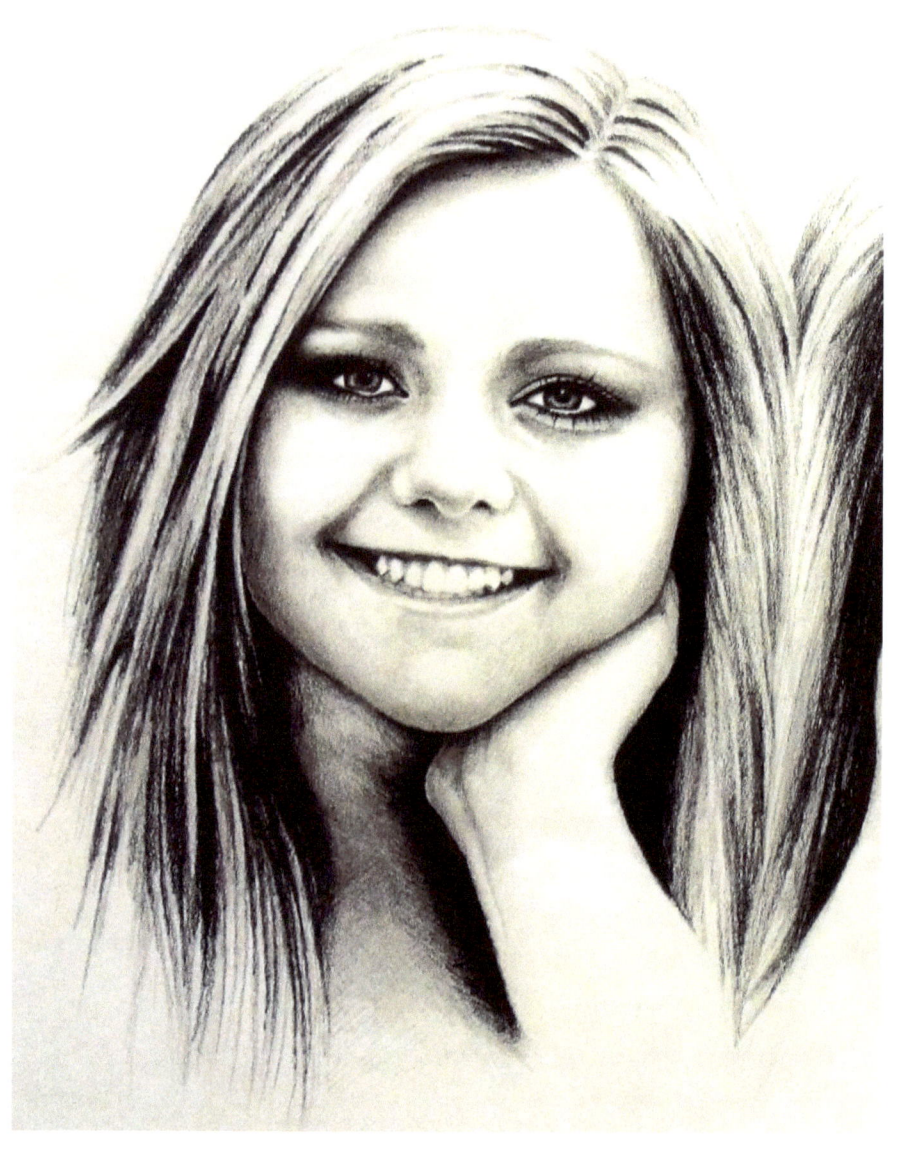

Close Up - A

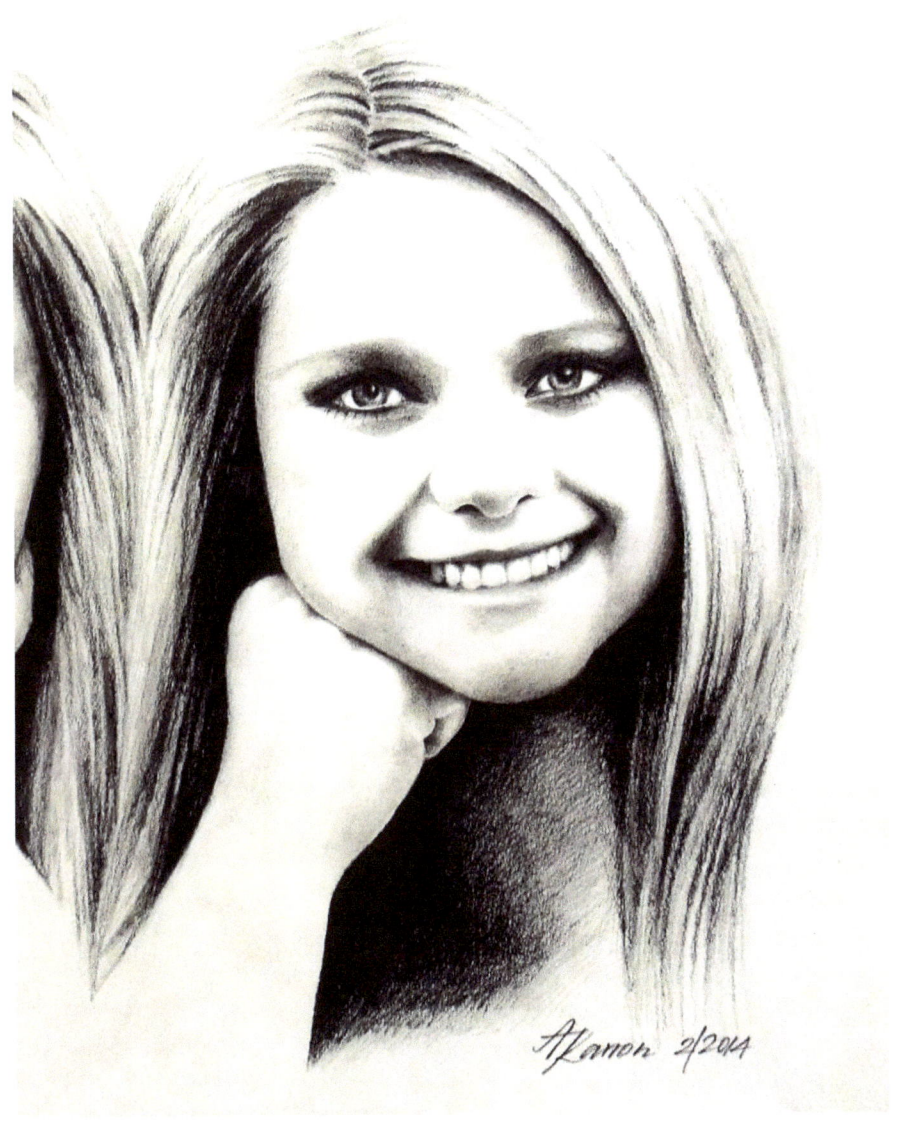

Close Up - B

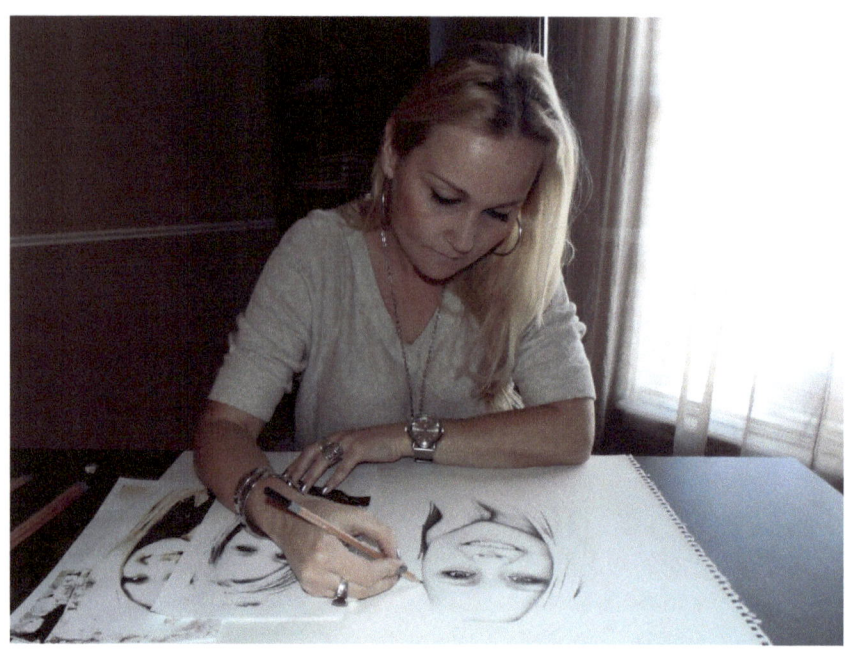

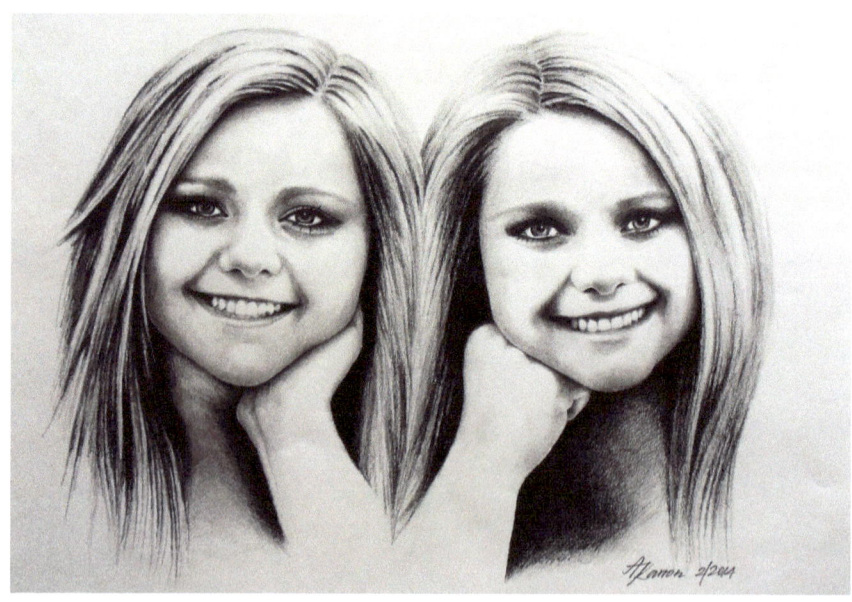

Finished Pencil Portrait – 2014

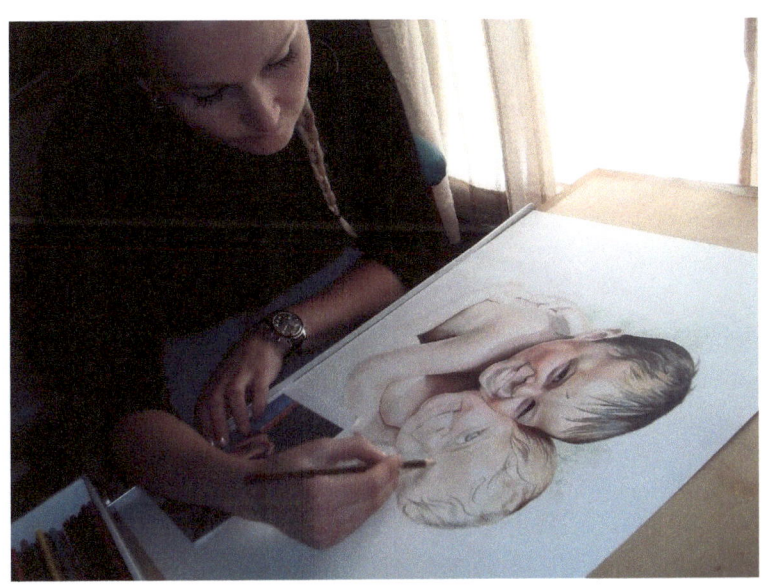

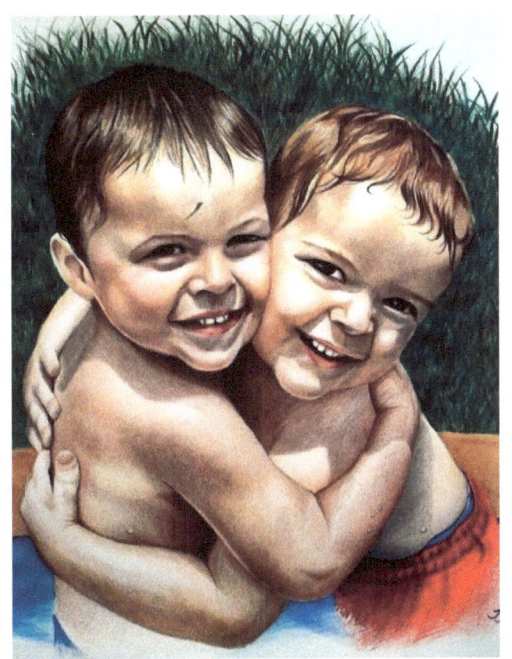

Finished Color Pencil Portrait - 2012

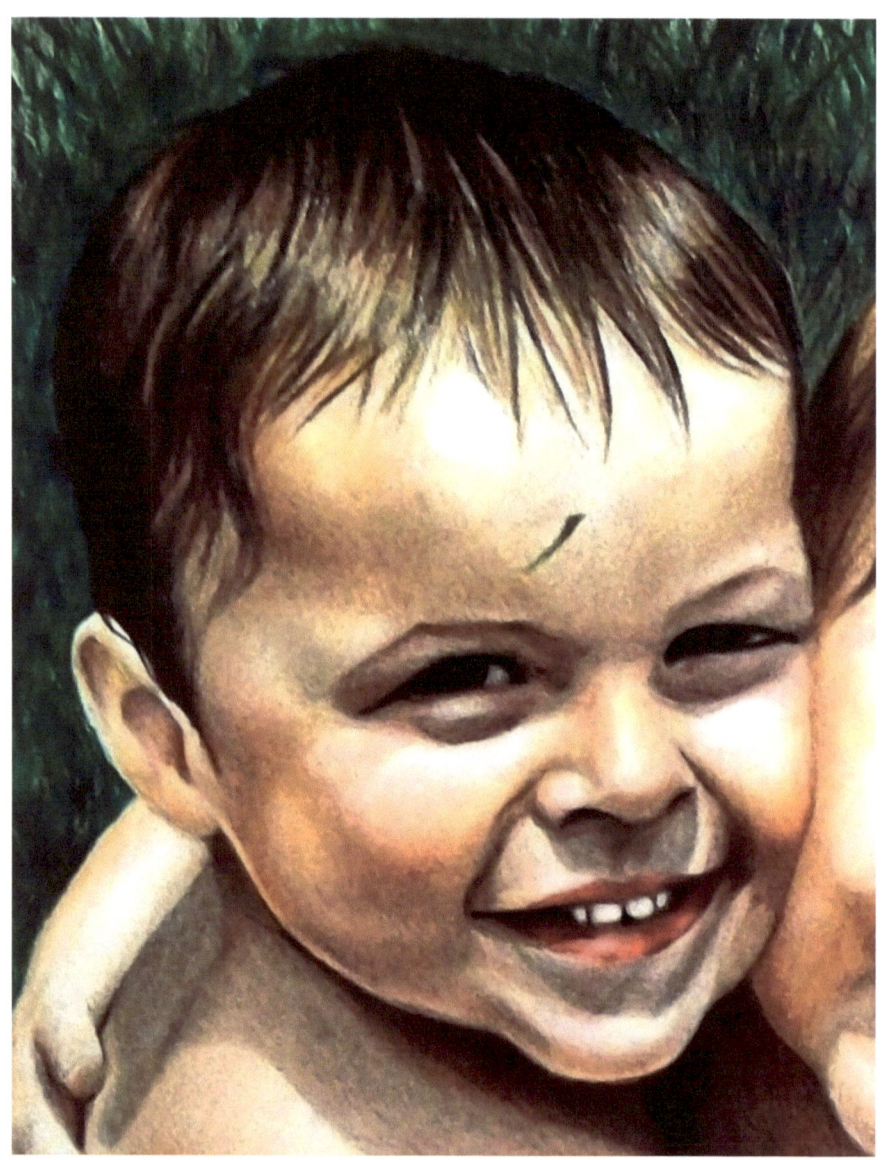

Close Up - A

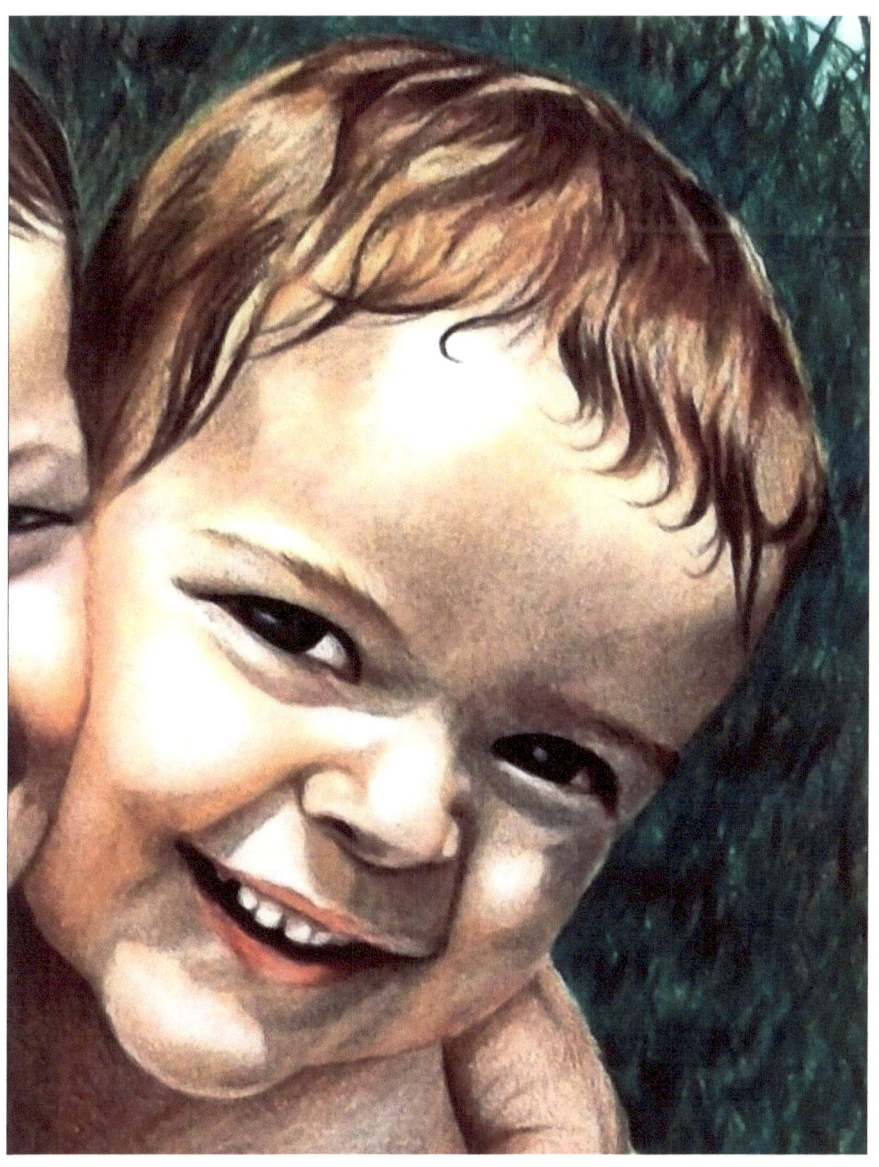

Close Up - B

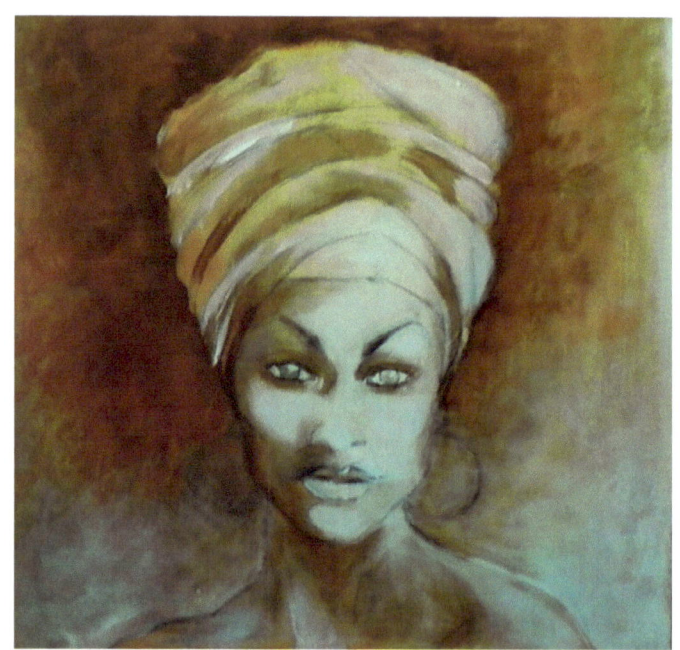
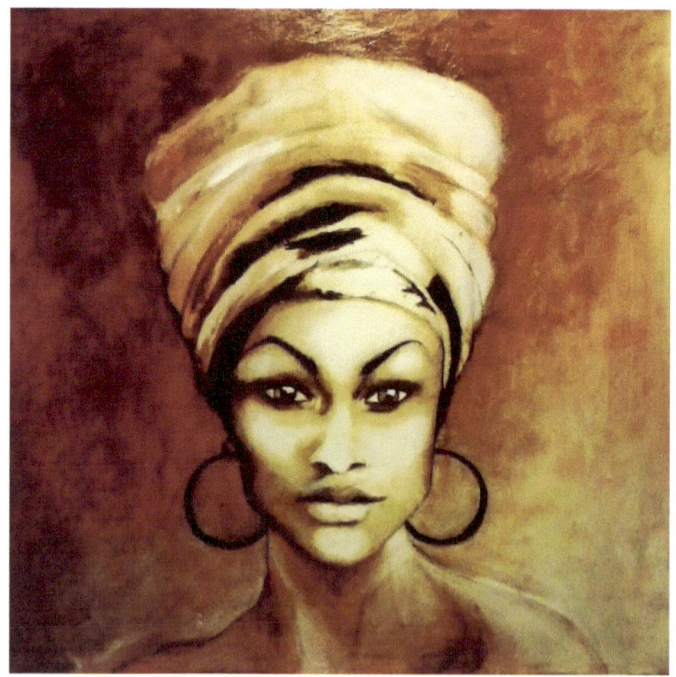

Work In Progress

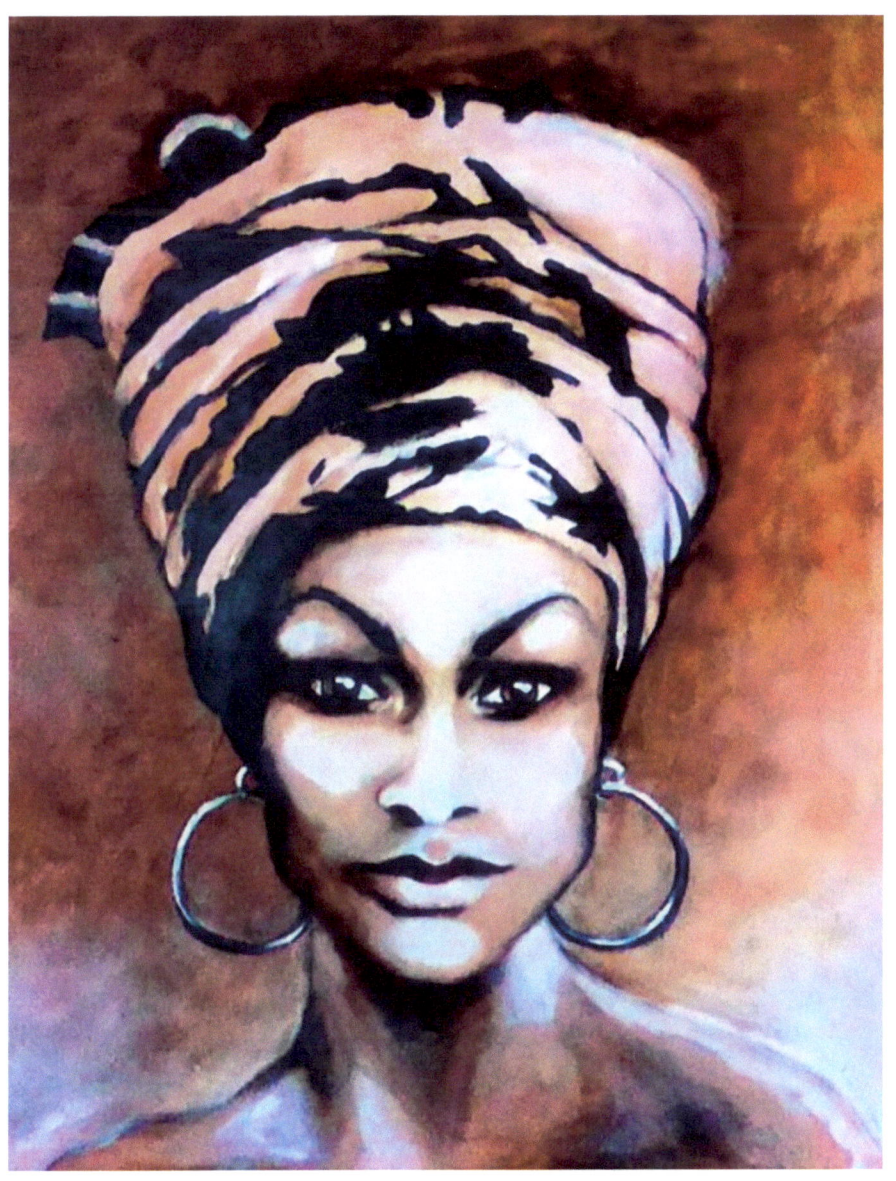

Finished Acrylic Painting – 2015

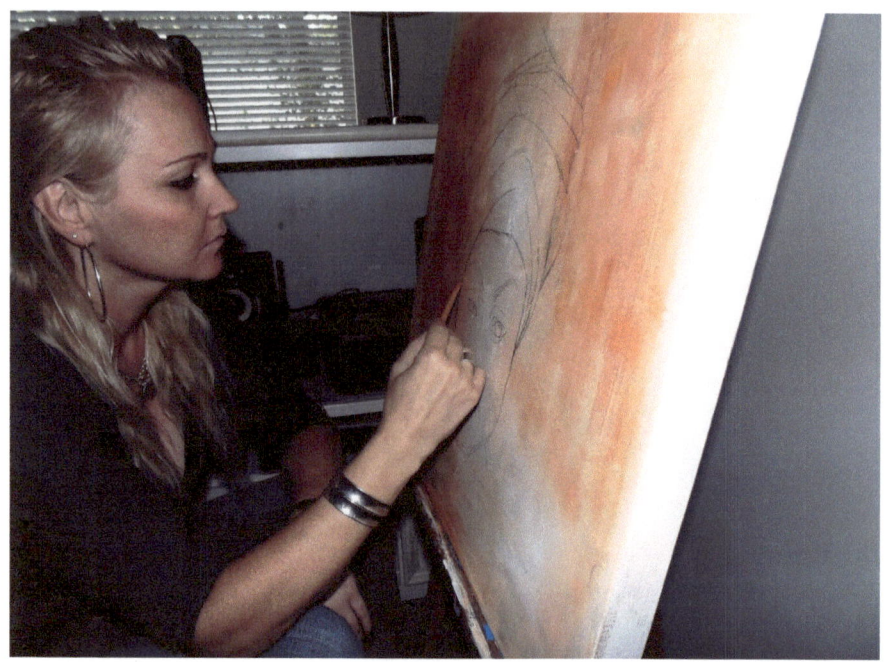

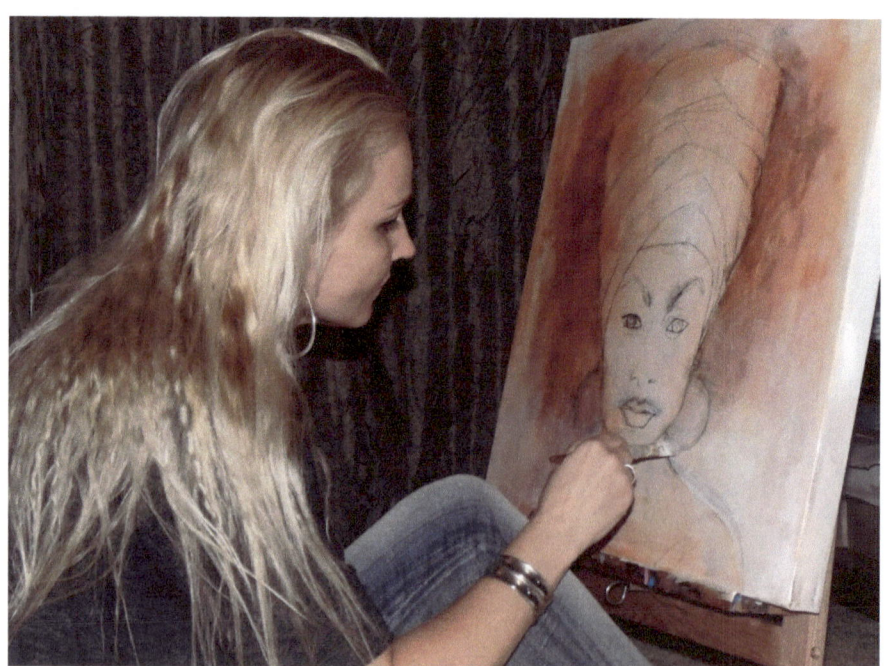

Work In Progress

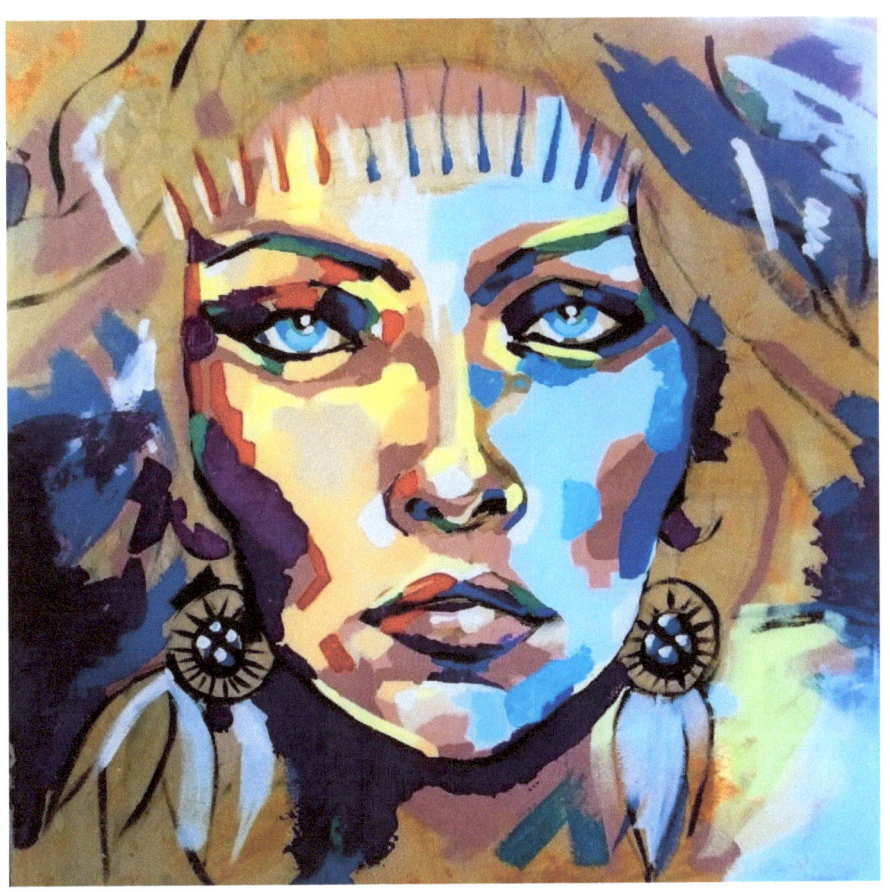

Acrylic Painting - 2018

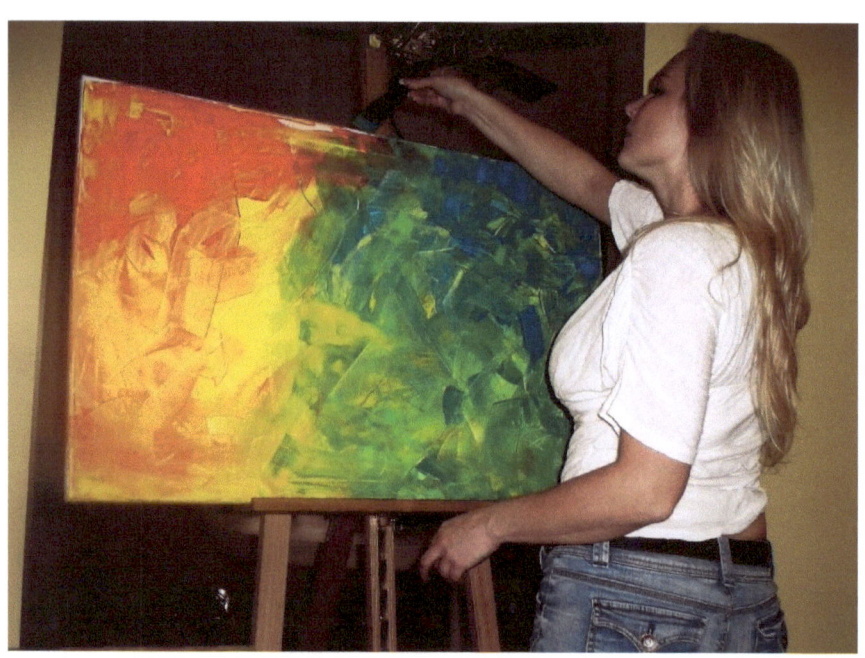

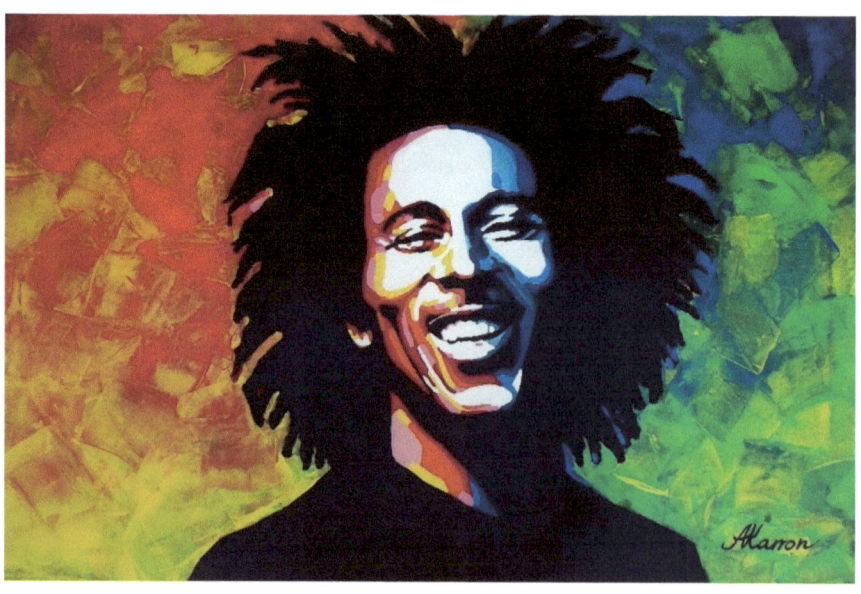

Finished Acrylic Painting - 2015

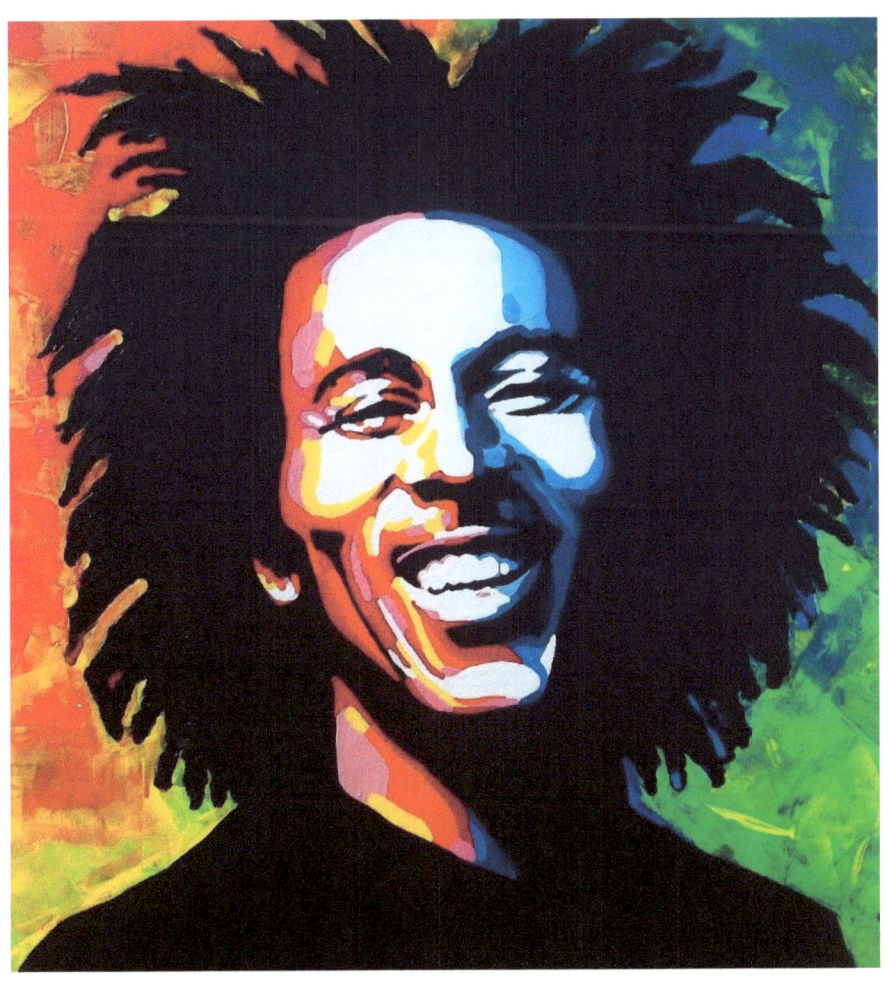

Acrylic Painting - 2015

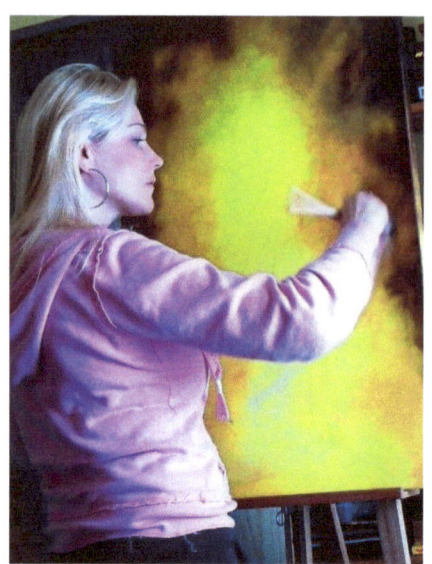
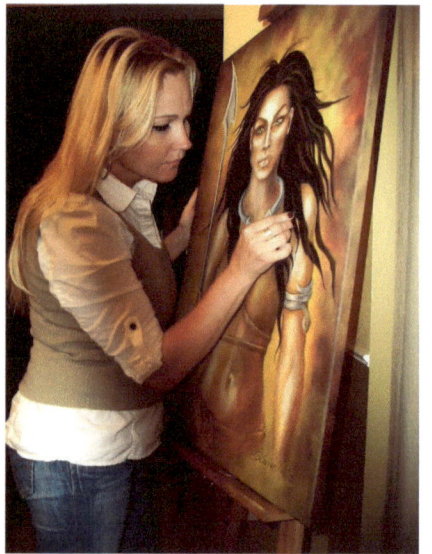
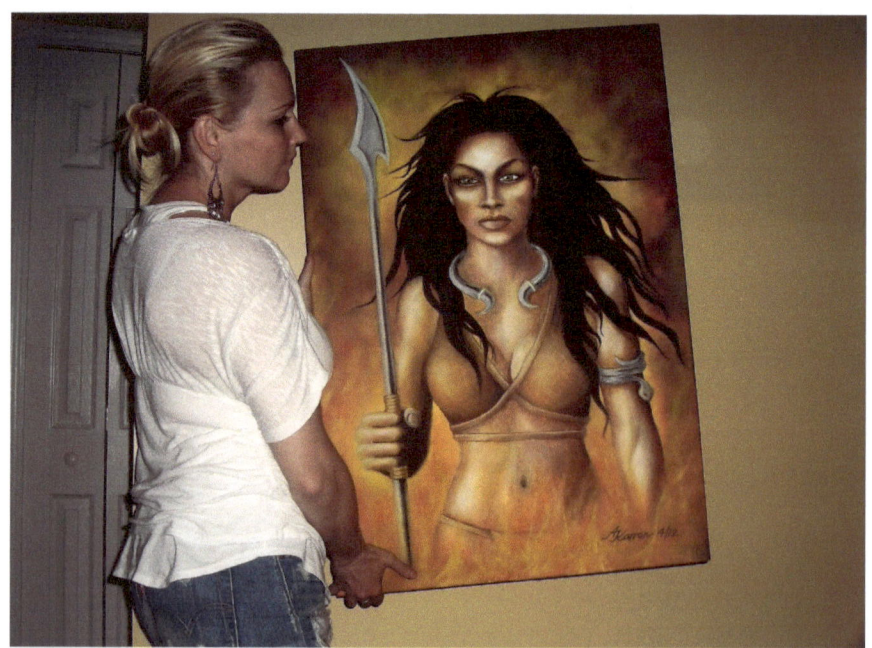

Work In Progress

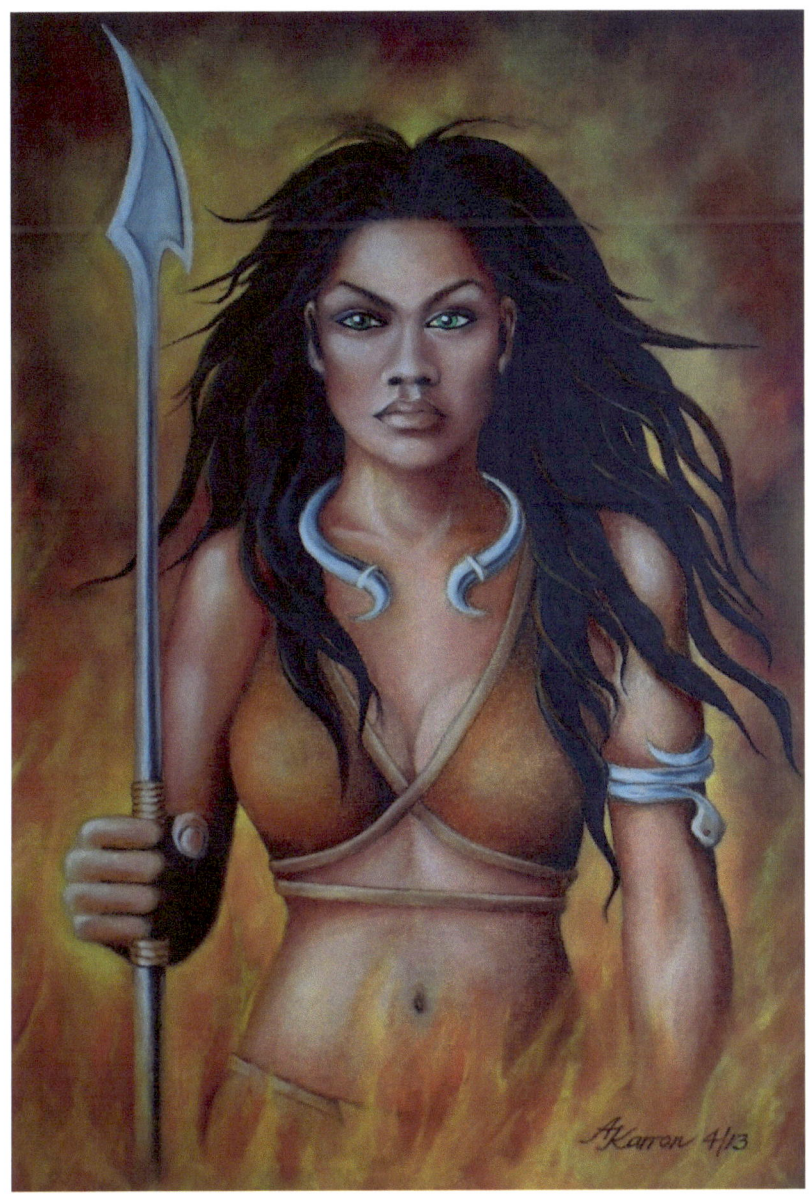

Finished Acrylic Paint and Oil Pastel – 2013

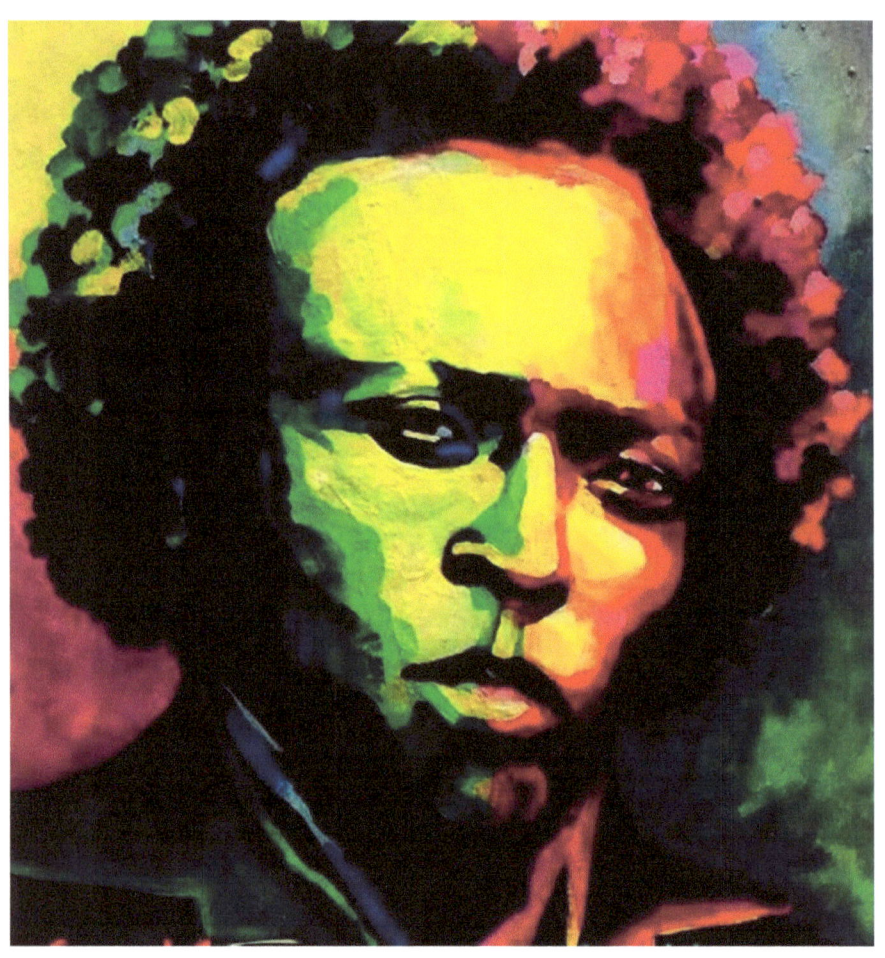

Acrylic Painting – 2015

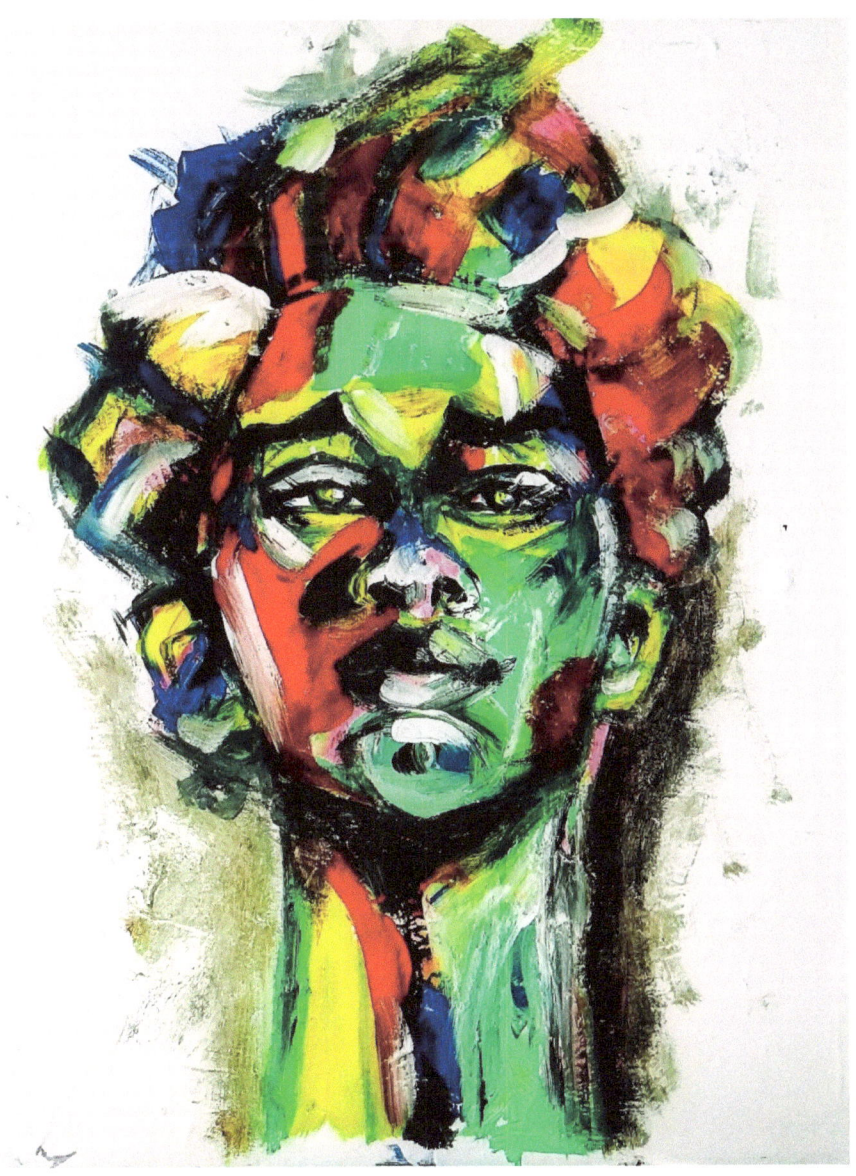

20-Minute Acrylic Painting - 2018

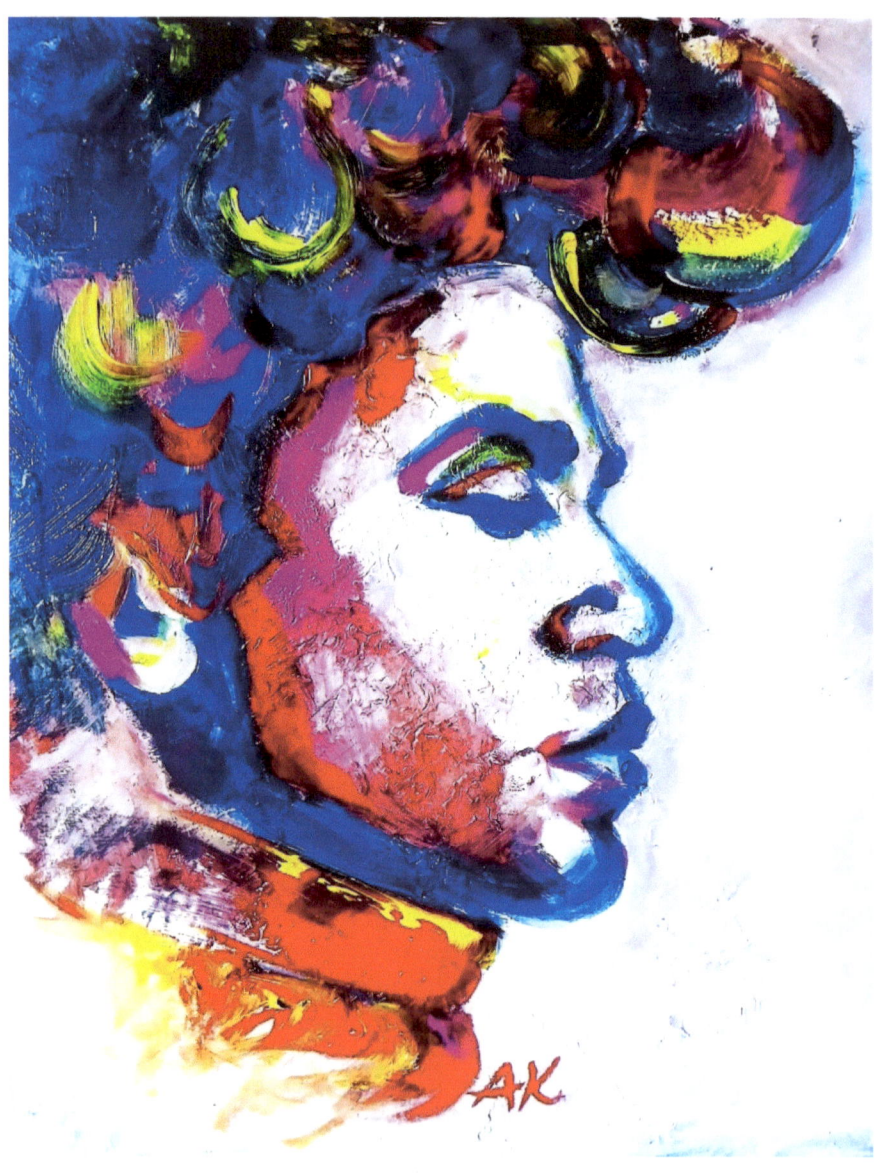

20-Minute Acrylic Painting – 2018

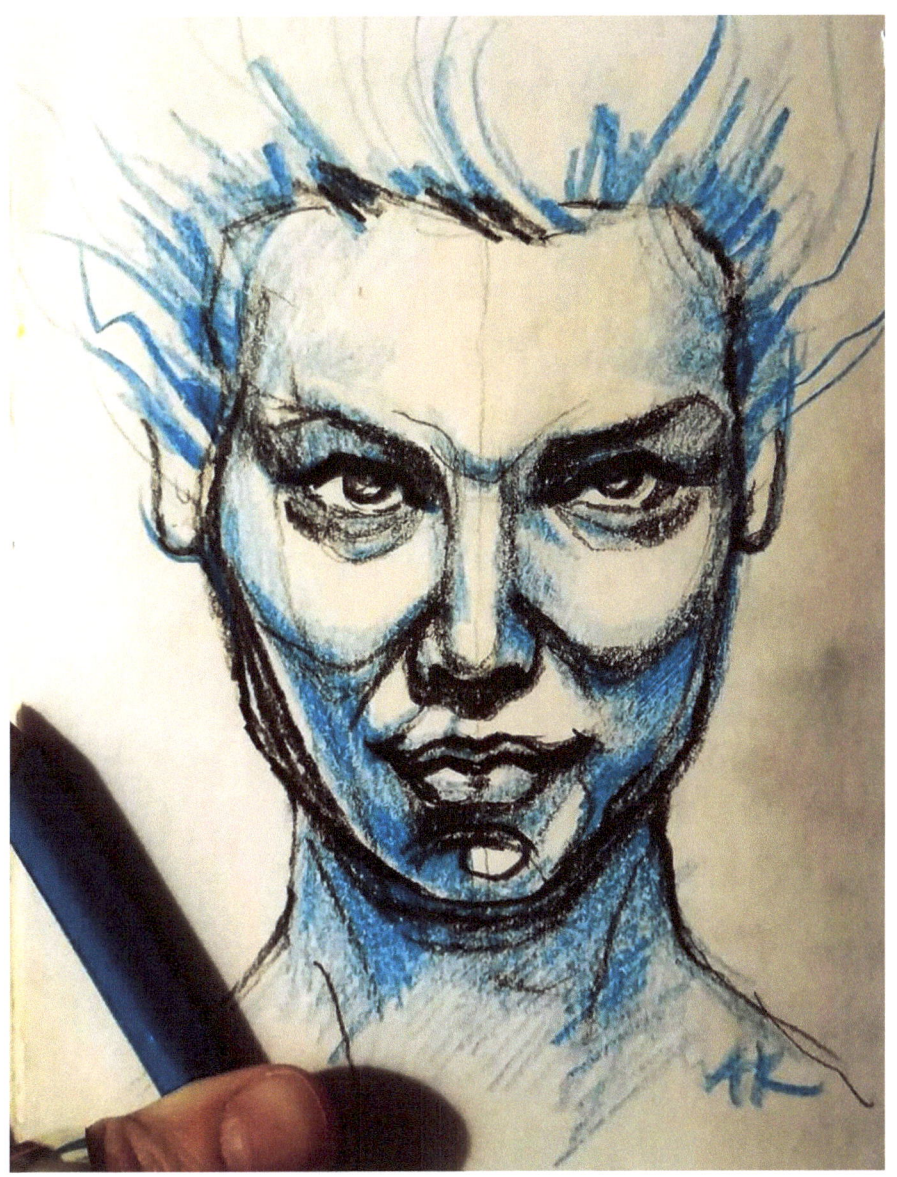

20-Minute Color Pencil Sketch – 2018

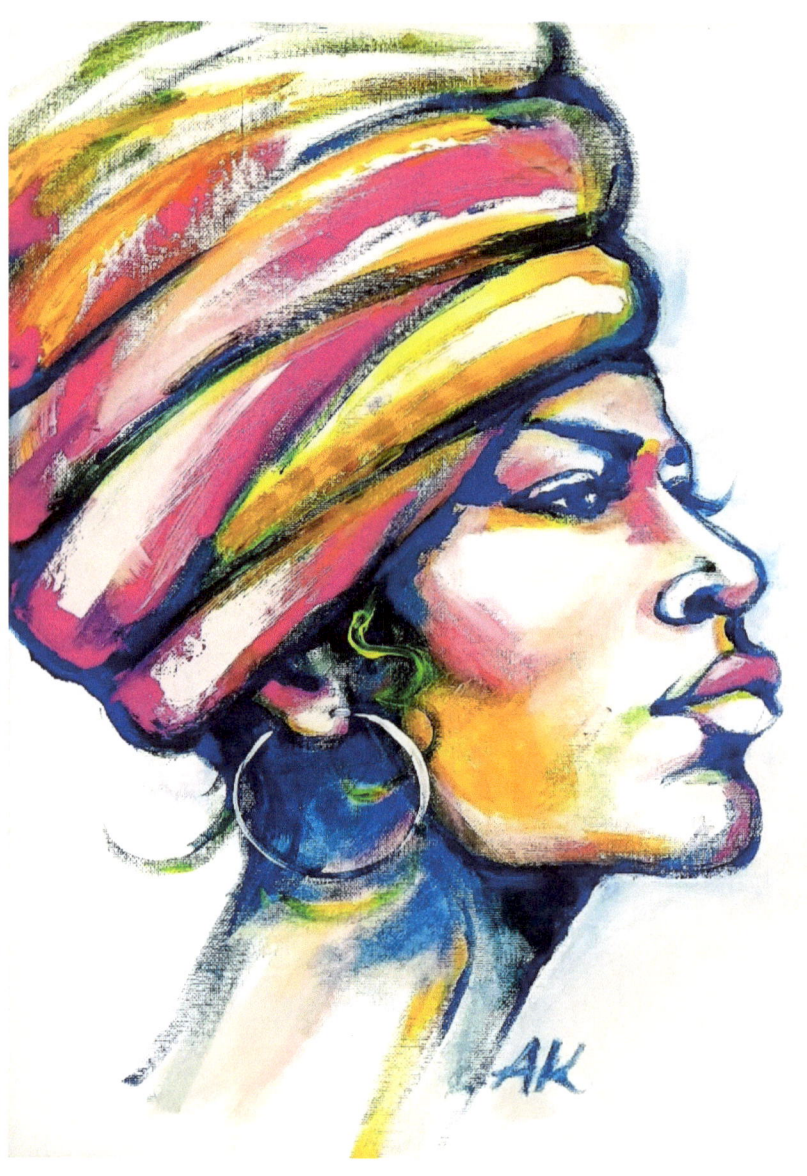

20-Minute Acrylic Painting – 2018

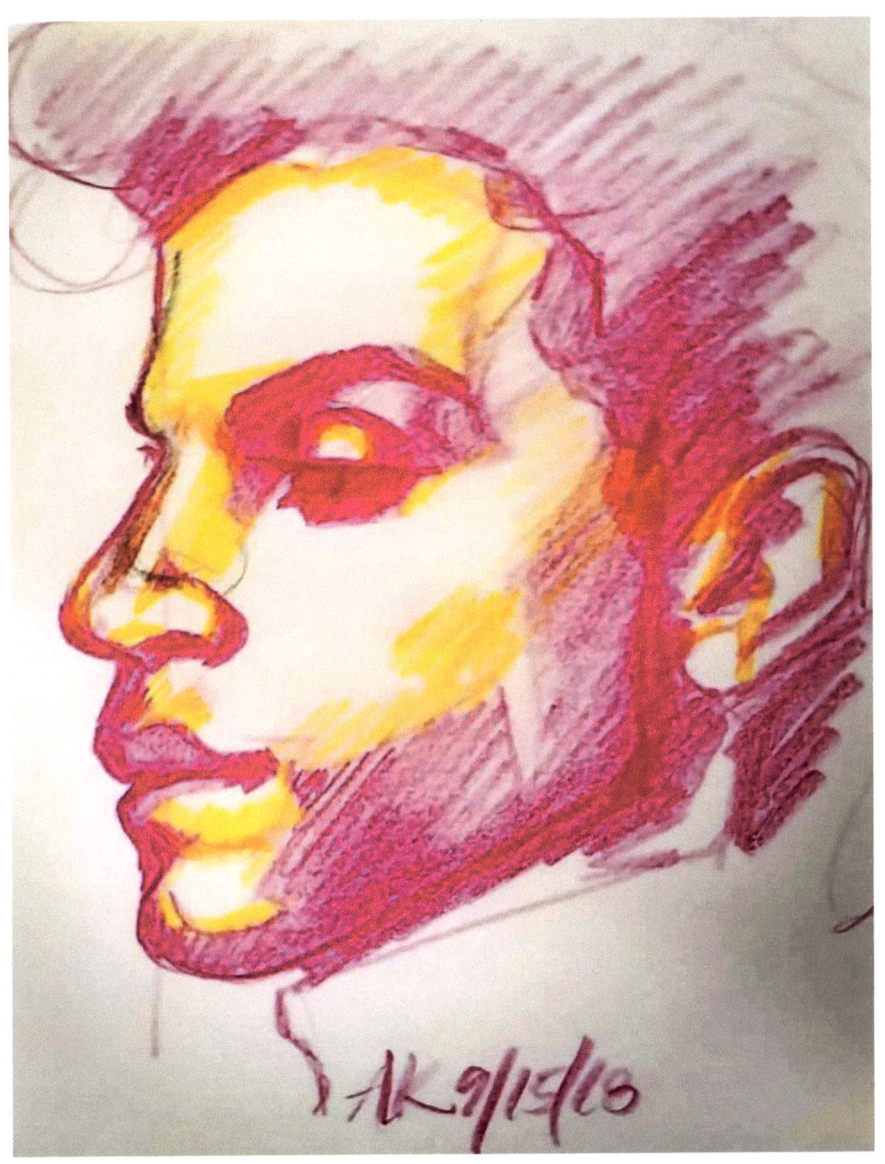

20-Minute Color Pencil Sketch – 2018

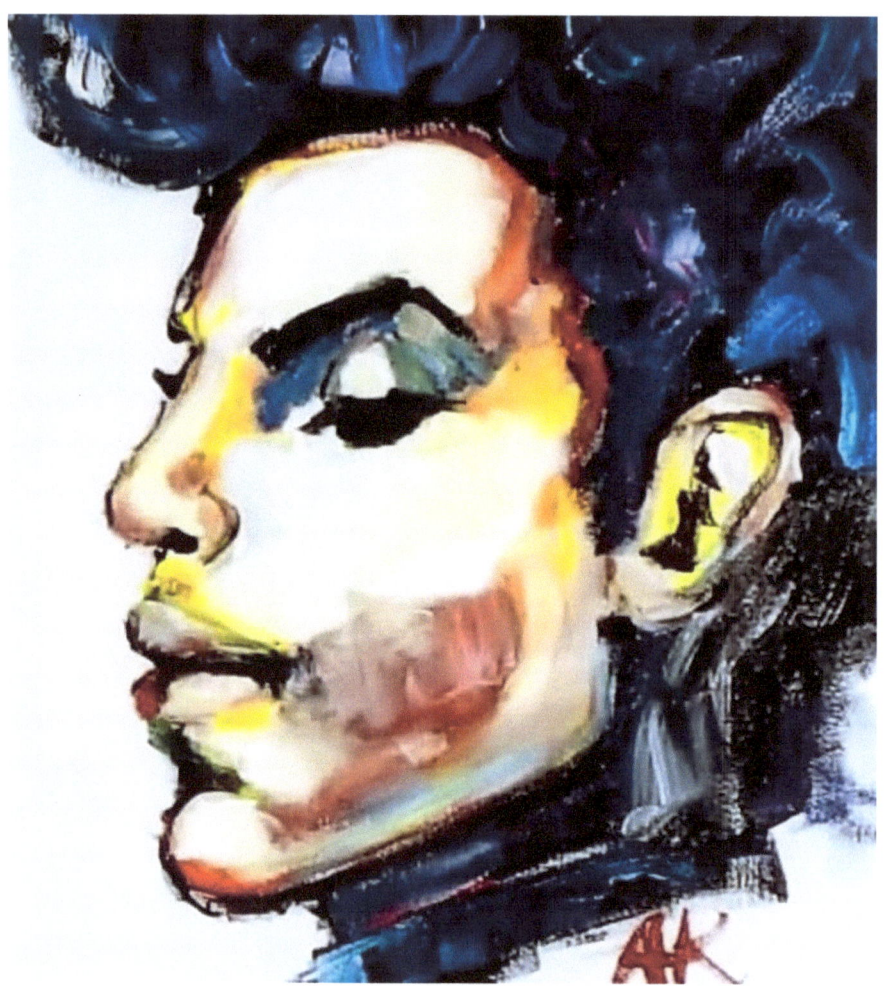

20-Minute Acrylic Painting - 2018

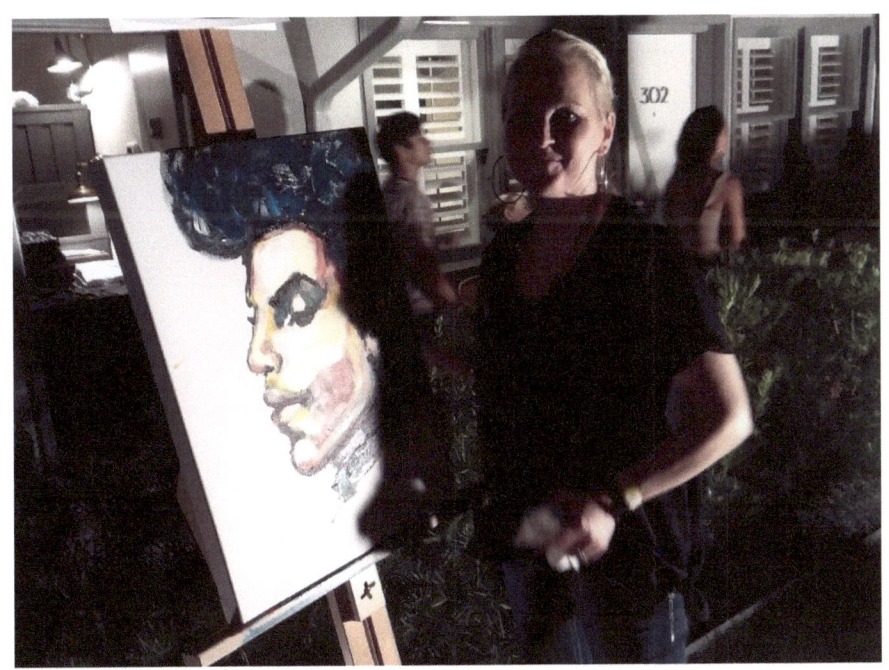

Art Battle - Jacksonville, FL
September 2018

www.ingramcontent.com/pod-product-compliance
Lightning Source LLC
Chambersburg PA
CBHW040244220526
45473CB00001B/366